DAY TRADING OPTIONS

How to Start Investing with the Ultimate and Practical Guide to Options Trading. Become a Smart Investor by Using Technical Analysis to Invest in Options (Beginners 2022 Guide)

Pat Howell

Table of Contents

Introduction

Before we get into some of the strategies associated with options trading, let us first review the fundamentals of stock options. You're probably aware of what a company's share or stock is. Currently in stock.A lot of things can happen during an exchange. You will notice that there will be many high-profile stocks that trade in large volumes. These may also have some derivatives associated with them. A derivative is a contract between at least two parties, and sometimes more, in which the value of the contract is derived from an underlying security, such as an index or a stock.Options and futures are the most commonly traded derivatives on the stock market. We won't spend much time on futures in this guidebook, but they are often easier to understand than options, but they have less flexibility and carry more risk.An option, on the other hand, is a type of contract that is sold by one party to another and gives the buyer the right, but not the obligation, to sell or buy an underlying stock at a predetermined price. These options usually come with an expiration date or time limit, and the buyer must decide what to do with it within that time frame. They can also work with the underlying asset at any time before the expiration date.

These options cannot exist indefinitely, and each has an expiration date. The option buyer will have the option to exercise their buyer at the time of expiry or before the expiry point. So, when would you rather use an option than rely on stocks?When you know that the underlying option's price will rise in the future, one option is to buy it. You can buy the option now, and then when the price rises, you can exercise your right to buy the stock at a lower price and then sell it for a profit.A good example of this is when a land developer is waiting to hear if new land regulations will be implemented. If the rules or regulations

If zoning rules are implemented, the price of that land will rise. The land developer and the landowner may enter into an options contract. This gives them the right, but not the obligation, to purchase the land by the end of the agreed-upon expiry date. As an incentive for the landowner to complete the contract, the land developer will be required to put some money down.If the regulations are passed, the land developer will agree to buy the land at a lower price. Their down payment will be applied to the amount they now owe. They never pay more than the contract amount, regardless of how much the land is worth at the time of purchase. Because they got such a good deal, the land developer can now build homes in that area and sell them for a good profit.

However, there is some risk involved in this. In the preceding example, if the regulations are not followed, the land developer may decide not to purchase the land. They do not have to complete the purchase, but they will have to forfeit the down payment they made earlier, so there is some financial loss in the situation.

Optional Structures

There are two types of options available to you when it comes to options. There will be telephone options. These will grant the buyer the right to purchase the contract's underlying security at a fixed price. This would be similar to the preceding example. There are also put options, which give the buyer the right to sell the underlying security at a fixed price.

The most important thing to remember when working with call options is that the buyer of the option can only begin to profit from it if the value of the underlying stock or index rises. In the case of a put option, however, the buyer can only begin to profit when the value of the underlying stock or index falls.

The Advantages and Disadvantages of Working with Options

We've spent some time researching options and learning about them. There will also be a plethora of strategies available to you if you decide to enter this market, and we will discuss them further as we go. However, you may be wondering why a trader would want to start in the options market at all. It appears to be more complicated than other forms of investing, and a new options trading investor may wonder if the risk is worth the long-term profits.

People choose to work in the options market as an investment option for a variety of reasons. First, an investor can profit from changes in an asset's market price without ever having to put money up to purchase that equity. They must pay a premium for that, but they are not required to pay the full price of the asset to enter the market. The required premium will be a fraction of the cost of what the investor would pay if they purchased the asset outright. This allows them to leverage their account more to enter a larger trade without having a large amount of capital, to begin with.

CHAPTER 1

What Exactly Is Options Trading

Here are two important ways to trade options. The first involves purchasing the option and speculating on the premium price. The premium's price will fluctuate depending on

how the underlying stock moves so that you can profit from it For example, if you believe a stock will rise, you can purchase an in-the-money call, and as the stock rises, so will its intrinsic value.

As a result, you benefit from the increase in the overall premium value. As the stock falls in value, the intrinsic value of the put rises, as does its premium. Remember that you're buying a put to profit from the price drop (not selling a put). The second method of speculating in options is to focus on the underlying rather than the premium.

What I mean is that you're far more concerned with exercising the option than with the underlying's price rise. This requires an additional step, but if you want to own the stock, this may be a better method to use. In general, many options traders do not bother exercising the contract because the premium tends to capture the intrinsic value change fairly well.

So far, it's been pretty straightforward, isn't it? Like common stock, you can swing or day trade options, but these methods require you to develop a directional bias in the markets. As we've seen, this raises your risk and isn't any different from normal trading activity. The point is that you do not need options to trade in this manner. So, how does one trade options wisely?

The best way to do this is to use the contract structure to isolate yourself from major market risk factors such as volatility. When swing or day trading, traders will frequently use what is known as a stop-loss order to limit their downside. On paper, this is a safety netbecause the market is prone to simply jumping the stop loss level during periods of high volatility.As a result, the trader faces larger-than-expected losses, and in some cases, such volatility may wipe out their entire account. Options avoid all of this drama because you will only pay the premium upfront, limiting your initial investment significantly. Then, you'll be using ironclad contracts to protect your downside, and the market won't be able to jump the price. Even if it does, your contract specifies the price, so you will always receive the stated price.

The Dangers of Option Trading

So far, I've only mentioned option trading based on the movements of the underlying stock. You buy a call if you believe it will rise. If you believe it will fall, buy a put. Can you short a call or a put? Yes, you can, and this is where the risks associated with options trading come into play.When you purchase an options contract, your risk is limited to the contract's terms. In exchange for selling you the contract, the person who sold it to you receives the premium. They will always have this premium. The writer is the person who sells the option.Writing options has their advantages. For starters, the vast majority of options traded expire out of the money. As a result, the writer keeps the option premium and usually does not have to worry about the contract being exercised. If the contract is exercised, it will cause a slew of problems. Consider the following scenario: if you've written a call (that is, sold it), and it moves into the money, your downside is limitless.

Keep in mind that when you write a call, you are betting that the underlying stock will not rise. If it does arise, it has the potential to reach infinity. What if your call's strike price is $10 and the stock rises to $10,000 before the expiration date? I know it's unlikely, but it's theoretically possible. The loss will easily exceed the equity in your account.

Writing a put does not have an infinite downside, but it does have a significant one. If the strike price of the put you wrote is $50, your profit is $50.The downside is a total loss of $50 per share (since the stock can decline only till 0). This is why writing options must be done with care.So, why do people write options in the first place, if the risks are so great? Apart from the fact that option writing usually results in a profit (via the premium earned), most option writers protect their downside by covering their option positions. So, when someone writes a call, they first purchase the underlying stock. Another option is to purchase a put at a lower strike price, which will protect them from the downside.You must be aware of the distinctions between writing options naked and writing them covered. Naked option writing is the riskiest thing you can do, and your broker will not let you do it. Covered writing is perfectly legal, and no broker will prevent you from doing so.

If you're wondering, once you've written an option, you can buy it back at a lower price before it expires. In other words, you can sell an option like a stock. Unless you change your trades, you won't need to do this with the strategies.Options have inherent leverage, and you should be aware of this. Because each contract represents ownership of 100 shares of the underlying stock, everything that occurs is multiplied by a factor of 100. This emphasizes the importance of flawlessly executing your strategies.

Aside from that, there are no risks associated with options. They lower your risk of trading in the market by reducing the effects of volatility. For directional traders, volatility is both a blessing and a curse. On the one hand, massive swings make their money. It's not so much fun when the swings flip over and wipe them out.

Accounts for Trading Options

You will need to open a brokerage account to trade options. You have a choice at this point. You can choose between a full-service broker and a discount broker. A full-service broker operates similarly to a financial supermarket. They have financial advisors on staff who can assist you with things like retirement planning, tax planning, and so on.A full-service brokerage will also have a selection of ETFs and mutual funds in which you can invest. People usually open their retirement accounts with full-service brokers because it gives them a sense of security. This, however, is a misunderstanding. Despite what the doomsday experts claim, the markets in the United States are extremely well regulated. You do not face fewer risks when working with a full-service broker than you would anywhere else. Full-service brokers charge higher commissions, and the only advantage of using one is that it makes it easier to connect your various accounts. If someone has a retirement account with one company, inertia causes them to open another with the same company, similar to how people usually stick with the same bank their entire lives (Pritchard, 2019).People make the mistake of believing that they will receive trading advice when they choose full-service brokers. Make no mistake about it: your broker is under no obligation to provide you with advice. Their fiduciary duty only extends to executing your trades as efficiently as possible. Your broker is not there to tell you which stocks will rise in value or which are the best investments for your retirement account.

They may have an army of CFAs on staff, but they are not permitted to recommend outside ETFs and products to their clients. The in-house funds always come with a higher fee. As a result, there is a significant conflict of interest. My point is, don't blindly trust your broker, especially if they employ CFAs. They don't give you unbiased investment advice, so why should they give you trading advice?

In general, keep in mind that your broker is not your friend. This is not to say they are your adversary, but they serve a specific purpose in the market, and it is their responsibility to carry it out. It is not to be used for anything else. It's similar to going to a florist and asking for bread. It's not their fault; it's the fault of those who have unrealistic expectations of their broker.This brings me to the topic of discount brokers. Discount brokerage firms are all about cutting costs and will only offer you one thing: execution. As a result, your commissions will be much lower. When it comes to trading, transaction costs are extremely important. Traders commonly believe that trading in the market is a zero-sum game. If one person wins, someone else loses the same amount. This is not correct. The broker profits regardless of what happens in the market. Your transaction costs are represented by a.You must overcome a stumbling block to profit. Consider the following scenario: suppose your broker charges you 0.1 percent per trade. So you pay 0.1 percent when you buy and 0.1 percent when you sell. Remember, whether you win or lose, this is the only thing that matters.As a result, to profit, each trade must earn at least 0.21 percent. It doesn't appear to be much. However, if you make 100 trades per year, you'll need to make 20% just to break even (0.2*100). Traders place 100 trades per month on average! So you can see how this hurdle rate adds up massively over time.This is why you should factor commissions into all of your profit and loss calculations. If you choose to risk a certain percentage of your account on a trade, you must account for the commission costs on the amount gained or lost. This advice applies to both directional and options traders, though the impact is much lower for options traders.

The fees charged by discount brokers vary depending on the type of trader they cater to. Fees for beginner-friendly platforms will be per leg or a fixed fee on a per-share basis, plus an additional fee because it involves an option transaction. Make sure you distinguish between per-share fees and contract fees.Some brokers quote prices for an entire contract, while others quote prices per leg, and so on. There is no standard procedure here. Simply choose the best platform and the lowest price. This invariably leads to traders opting for Interactive Brokers. Light speed is another excellent platform, but it is geared toward more advanced and active options traders, so I would not recommend it for beginners.

CHAPTER 2

How Does Day Trading Work

Always remember the first rule of day trading: never hold a position overnight, even if it means losing trades.But why do you have to follow this rule even if it means losing money in the market? After all, isn't the goal of day trading to make money?Yes, the goal of day trading is to make money. However, because the best securities for day trading are volatile, holding them overnight puts you at risk of suffering significant losses the next day. When you try to hold on today trading securities overnight in the hopes that prices will recover significantly the next day, it's better to take small losses on day trades than large ones.You can minimize day trading losses by closing your position at the end of the day, even if it is a loss. And if you can close positions at a profit, that's fantastic! Don't think you'll be able to earn more money if you wait until tomorrow. Remember, a bird in hand is worth three in the bush.

You should also keep in mind that trading is not the same as regular investing. While trading is a type of investing, regular investing is a more passive, buy-and-hold strategy that waits months or years before taking profits. Trading has a much shorter time frame, which is only a couple of months at most for swing trading and several hours for day trading.

Investing in Long-Term Assets and Selling Short-Term Assets

When you purchase financial security, you are assuming a long position in that security. When a trader says he or she is long 100 shares of Intel stock, it means that the trader purchased and is currently holding 100 shares of Intel stock.The purpose of taking a long position in financial security is to sell it later at a higher price. To close a long position, you sell the securities that you own.

When you sell securities that you do not yet own, you are taking a short position in those securities. When a trader says he or she shorted or sold short 100 shares of Intel stock, it means that the trader sold 100 shares of Intel stock in the hopes that the price will continue to fall so that he or she can repurchase it at a much lower price. It's the same concept as buying low and selling high, except the "selling high" part comes before the "buying low."

How can you sell something you don't have, and even more importantly, why would you?

First, let us discuss why you should do so. And the answer is: to profit when the value of securities falls. As previously stated, it is simply a reversal of the general trading strategy of purchasing securities at low prices and selling them at higher prices. You can trade profitably even during market downturns by selling securities at high prices and buying them later at lower prices.How are you going to do it now? You can borrow securities from your broker, sell them, repurchase them when prices fall, and return the securities you borrowed from your broker, depending on your broker and whether you are qualified. You profit from the short sale in the process.Keep in mind, however, that short selling, like long positions, has risks, including the possibility that prices will rise instead of continuing to fall. You may also incur trading losses in this case.

You might be wondering why brokers or exchanges would lend securities to their clients for short selling rather than sell the securities themselves. That's a great question. And the answer is that brokers are typically interested in taking long-term positions on securities. Why?Why take risks with short-term trades in a downtrending market when they can make much more money by simply lending it to customers who want to short sell for a fee? Everyone benefits in this manner. Long-term investors can keep their securities and profits even during bear markets.Short-selling provides opportunities for those who do not own securities to make profitable trades.

Retail Traders vs. Institutional Traders

Retail traders are individuals who trade on a part-time or full-time basis but do not work for a firm and do not manage other people's money. These traders control a small portion of the trade market's volume.Institutional traders, on the other hand, are made up of hedge funds, mutual funds, and investment banks that are often armed with advanced software and typically engage in high-frequency trading.

Human involvement in the operations of investment firms is now quite limited. Institutional investors, backed by professional analysts and large investments, can be quite aggressive.So, at this point, you may be wondering how a newcomer like you can compete with the big boys.

Our benefit is the freedom and flexibility we have. Institutional traders are required by law to trade. Individual traders, in the meantime, are free to trade or refrain from trading if the market is currently volatile.Regardless of the stock price, institutional traders should be active in the market and trade large volumes of stocks. Individual traders are free to sit out and trade if opportunities arise in the market.

Unfortunately, most retail traders lack the knowledge to determine when it is best to be active and when it is best to wait. To be profitable in day trading, you must overcome greed and cultivate patience.The biggest issue with day traders is not the size of their accounts or a lack of access to technology, but rather a lack of discipline. Many people are prone to poor money management and excessive trading.Some retail traders are successful by employing the guerilla strategy, which refers to the unconventional trading approach derived from guerilla warfare. Guerilla combatants are skilled at manipulating a more visible and less mobile conventional opponent through hit-and-run tactics such as raids, sabotage, and ambushes.Keep in mind that your goal is not to defeat institutional traders. Instead, concentrate on waiting for the right opportunity to earn your desired income.You can profit from market volatility as a retail trader. When the markets are flat, it can be difficult to make money. Only institutional traders have the resources, expertise, and capital to gamble in such situations.

You must learn how to select stocks that will allow you to make quick decisions to the downside or upside in a predictable manner. Institutional traders, on the other hand, practice high-frequency trading, which allows them to profit from minor price movements.But, in a nutshell, Alpha Predators are what retail traders are looking for. These stocks typically tank when the markets are rising and rise when the markets are falling.It is generally acceptable if the market and the stocks are both running. Just make sure you're trading stocks that are moving because they have a valid reason to move and aren't simply reacting to market conditions.

You're probably wondering what the necessary catalyst for stocks is for them to be suitable for day trading.

- Here are some examples of catalysts:

- Debt sacrifices Buybacks Splitting of stocks

- Management shifts Restructuring and layoffs

- Contract wins/losses that are significant Partnerships/alliances

Important product launches Acquisitions and/or mergers FDA approval/rejection Surprising earnings Earnings statements

Retail traders who engage in reversal trades typically select stocks that are selling off as a result of negative press about the company. When there is a rapid sell-off due to negative press, many traders will notice and begin monitoring the stock for what is known as a bottom reversal.

How can you spot the stocks that are enticing retail investors? There are some tried-and-true methods for accomplishing this.To begin, you can employ day trading stock scanners. Retail traders are primarily interested in stocks that are significantly moving up or down at price.Second, look for online community groups or social media groups for retail traders. Twitter and Stock Twits are frequently good places to learn about current trends. If you follow successful traders regularly, you will be able to see for yourself what everyone is following. Being a part of a day trading community has a significant advantage.

Securities at Risk

There's a reason why so many investors, traders, and analysts pay attention to market movements or indices. It's because they understand that, in general, most financial securities will follow the overall trend of their respective markets unless they have compelling reasons not to. For example, when the Dow Jones is trending upward, the prices of most NYSE stocks tend to rise, and vice versa.However, for one reason or another, there will always be outliers.

—defy the general trend for a specific reason. They are picking up when their general markets are tanking. They are tanking at a time when their general markets are improving.These are known as securities in play (SIP). These are the securities you should concentrate on as a retail or individual day trader in your chosen day trading market.

These are stocks to day trade if you want to deviate from the general trend of the NYSE or NASDAQ. If futures contracts are used, they will be against the general direction of most other similar agreements.

You get the idea, don't you? Right!

What are some of the possible explanations for SIPs' contrarian behavior? These could include:

Earnings results that were not expected;Surprising corporate or economic developments; and Significant policy changes by the ruling authorities.So, just because security deviates from the general market trend does not imply that it is a SIP. The contrarian movement should be motivated by something. If there are none, it is most likely not a SIP.Another important day trading rule to remember, especially when selecting SIPs to day trade: Determine whether the movement of a specific security is due to general market sentiment or a unique fundamental reason.

You'll need to do your homework for this. As a beginner day trader, you may need to do a little more research than usual. However, as you gain experience as a day trader, you'll be able to tell when security is simply following the general market trend and when it's trending for a unique and specific reason.

Professional day traders are those who make a living from this type of trading. While other types of trading can be done as a hobby or to get a gambling high, day trading is frequently excluded. You will most likely lose money if you do not understand the market and its fundamentals.

CHAPTER 3

Strategies for Basic Options

To get started trading options quickly, you must first understand the fundamental options strategies. Options trading can be confusing at times, to the point where you may not even know when to enter.

and leave the market However, this is simply due to a lack of understanding of the fundamental options trading strategies.After you understand the fundamentals of how options work, as well as market trends, moods, and emotions, you must clarify your strategies. Starting with basic strategies is a good place to start for newcomers. Before moving on to more complex, advanced, and sophisticated trading strategies, you should ensure that you are a master of the fundamentals.

Even if you have a good understanding of the fundamentals of your options, you should go over them again until you are confident in them. In general, options trading is a two-way street. One party is selling, while the other is purchasing. Stocks or other financial instruments are not sold here. The seller is selling the right to buy or sell an asset that he or she owns at a specified price within a specified time frame.Even though most people associate options trading with stocks, it encompasses much more. Other financial instruments are traded in the financial market using options. Stocks, bonds, indexes, ETFs, commodities, currencies, futures, and other derivatives are examples of these. The securities or derivatives may differ, but the same trading principles apply in all cases.

Trading Strategies: Bearish, Bullish, and Neutral

The stock market is constantly in motion. To make money in the market, a trader must first analyze the moods and trends of the marketwhen the market will move upwards or downwards Various options strategies can be used based on these decisions.To be successful in the stock market, you must first understand market trends and stock movements, and then use that knowledge to predict when to strike. Instead of simply entering the stock market and buying a stock outright, which can result in a loss if the stock price falls, you can use bearish and bullish options strategies to profit while still managing your risk and trading capital.

Trading Strategies for The Upside

If you believe that the value of a security will rise as a result of your fundamental and technical analysis, you will employ a bullish trading strategy. The underlying security could be a stock/index or anything else. Profits from bullish trading strategies can be made by trading options with the expectation that the price of a stock (the underlying security) will rise. If your predictions come true, you will have a chance to profit from that analysis.

It may not even be a prediction in the movement of the stock price; it may be that you realized that the market is likely to move upward at a specific point in time and then used an options trading strategy to capitalize on that analysis. Buying a call option is the best bullish trading strategy in general.When you purchase a call option, you profit when the stock price rises above the strike price during the contract's specified period. In this case, your options trading is profitable. It is important to note that your profit is made if the call option is "in the money" at the time of the contract. This ensures that you make a reasonable profit from the increase in security above the strike price of the options contract. If your prediction does not come true at the time of the call option contract, you will lose money.

Purchasing a Protective Put

A protective put is another way to profit from a bullish options trading strategy. Market volatility and uncertainty can cause an owner to lose money.Consider using a put option to protect and hedge your stock shares. A put option allows a stockholder to protect his investment against price declines, allowing him to maintain a long-term position in the stock.The owner of that stock has "insured" it against losses by paying a price known as a "put premium." If the stock price falls rather than rises, the owner of the put option may profit from the transaction. However, if the stock rises slightly above the strike price, the trader may lose on the put trade because the put option may be required.

Trading Strategies for the Bears

Do you believe the price of an underlying security will fall? If you're going to bet on the market based on this analysis, the best approach to take is to use bearish options trading strategies. You hope to profit from this strategy if the stock price falls below the strike price of your options contract on or before the expiration date. When this occurs, you have a chance of making a profit.

If your analysis shows that the market will experience a drop in an underlying security, you can employ a variety of strategies. Among these strategies are the following: Long Put and Put Back spreads are two types of spreads. Bear Put Spread and Covered Put are the best strategies to use if you expect the market to fall just slightly above its current level. While Naked Calls are also good, the risk associated with this trading method can be very high if you are new to the options trading market.

You must understand that the market can sometimes outperform your forecast. When the market rises rather than falls, you may lose money on your stock options trading. As a result, you must consider all other factors before making trading analyses and decisions.A Put Option in a bearish trading strategy is slightly different from the one used in a bullish trading strategy. In a protection put option, you own the underlying stock, but you are attempting to hedge the stock against losses due to market uncertainty. APut-call options, on the other hand, imply that you do not own the underlying stock at the time of the contract. By writing the option, you are opening the market in this case.

Strategies for a Neutral Option

When you want to predict that there will be no significant changes in the stock market, you use a neutral trading strategy. For example, suppose you performed technical analysis and also considered the key fundamental events affecting an underlying stock, and you conclude that the company's stock will remain stable. If a company's stock is expected to remain stable due to market conditions, a neutral options strategy is the best option to use.

There is less volatility in neutral market analysis, so the movement of the stock price in the financial market remains stagnant. Ratio spreads, Strangles, Straddles, and Condors are some of the techniques to use in the case of these events.

CHAPTER 4

Styles and Varieties of Options

Regardless of the style or strategy an options day trader employs, he or she must always consider three critical factors. These are the elements:

Liquidity: This metric describes how quickly an option or other asset can be bought and sold without affecting the current market price. Because they trade more easily, liquid options are more appealing to options day traders. The ease with which a trader can open or close a position is hampered by illiquid options. This increases the time required to complete the transactions involved, which can result in a loss for the options day trader.

Volatility describes how sensitive the assets associated with the options are to price changes caused by external factors. Some assets have higher volatility than others. Stocks and cryptocurrencies are highly volatile investments. Volatility has a significant impact on the profit margin of an options day trader.

Volume refers to the number of options traded during a given period. Because volume is a gauge of the asset's interest in the market, it is an indicator of the associated asset's price movement on the market. The higher the volume, the more interested traders are in pursuing an option. Volume is one of the components of open interest, which is the total number of active options. There are no active options that have been liquidated, exercised, or assigned. If an options trader fails to act on options for an extended period, the situation may become unfavorable, resulting in unneeded losses. An options trader must always be on the lookout for opportunities to close options positions at the right time.To take advantage of the day trading options listed below, the day trader must be very familiar with these factors and how to use them to his or her advantage.

Day Trading Options on a Breakout

The term "breakout" refers to the process of entering the market when prices move outside of their normal price range. For this type of trading to be successful, there must be an increase in volume. There are several types of breakouts, but we will focus on one of the most common, known as support and resistance breakouts.

The support and resistance method describes the point at which the associated asset price ceases to decrease (support) and the point at which the associated asset price ceases to increase (resistance) (resistance). If the associated asset price breaks above resistance, the day trader will enter a long position. The options day trader, on the other hand, will enter a short position if the associated asset falls below the supported price. As you can see, the trader's position is determined by whether the asset is supported or resisted at the new price level. Volatility typically rises as the asset surpasses the normal price barrier. This usually results in the associated asset's price moving in the direction of the breakout.When considering this trading style, the options day trader must carefully consider his or her entry and exit points. The typical entry strategy is determined by whether the prices are set to close above or below the resistance level. If the price is said to be above the resistance level, the day trader will take a bearish position. If prices are expected to close below the support, a bullish approach is typical.Exit strategies necessitate a more refined approach. To determine a price target to close his or her position, the options day trader must consider past performance and chart patterns. When the target is met, the day trader can exit the trade and enjoy the profit.

Day Trading Momentum Options

This options day trading style describes the process of trading options based on price volatility and volume rate of change. It is so-called because the strategy's central premise is that the force driving the price movement of the associated asset is sufficient to keep it moving in the same direction. This is because when the price of an asset rises, it typically attracts investors, driving the price even higher. Options day traders who use this strategy profit from the expected price movementby riding the momentum.This strategy is based on using technical analysis to track the price movement of the underlying asset. This analysis provides the day trader with a comprehensive picture that includes momentum indicators such as:

The Momentum Indicator determines the strength of a price movement as a trend by using the most recent closing price of the associated asset.

The Relative Strength Index (RSI), which compares profits and losses over a specified time.Moving averages allow a day trader to see past fluctuations to analyze market trends.

The Stochastic Oscillator compares the most recent closing prices of the associated asset over a specified period.Momentum options day trading is highly effective and simple when done correctly. To make informed decisions using this trading style, the day trader must stay current on news and earnings reports.

Day Trading Reversal Options

This strategy is based on trading against the trend and is essentially the inverse of momentum options day trading. It is performed when an options day trader can identify pullbacks against the current price movement trends. It is also known as trend trading or pull-back trending. This is a risky move, but it can be quite profitable if everything goes as planned. Because of the depth of market knowledge and trading experience required to execute this style effectively, it is not one that beginners should try.This is a bullish approach to options trading that involves purchasing an out-of-the-money call option and selling an out-of-the-money put option. Profit and loss are both potentially limitless.

Day Trading Options Scalping

The process of buying and selling the same associated asset several times in the same day is referred to as options day trading. This is profitable when the market is extremely volatile. The options day trader makes money by purchasing an option position at a lower price and then selling it at a higher price, or by selling an option position at a higher price and then purchasing it at a lower price, depending on whether the option is a call or a put option.

This type of options trading relies heavily on liquidity. Illiquid options should not be used with this strategy because the options day trader must be able to open and close these types of trades several times in a single day. Trading liquid options allow the day trader to maximize profits when entering and exiting trades.Rather than trying to trade large amounts of money infrequently, the typical strategy is to trade several small options throughout the day to accumulate profit. Trading big with this style can result in massive losses in a matter of hours. This is why, despite being a less risky method, this style is only recommended for disciplined options day traders who are content with seeking small, repeated profits.

Because of the nature of this trading style, it is the shortest form of options day trading because it does not even last the entire day—only a few hours. Scalpers are day traders who trade in this manner. Technical analysis is required to determine the best bets based on the price movement of the underlying assets.Scalping is a broad term that refers to a variety of scalping techniques. There is time and sales scalping, in which a day trader uses records of bought, sold, and canceled transactions to determine the best options to trade and when the best times to trade are. Other types of scalping involve the use of bars and charts to forecast the direction of the market.

The Use of Pivot Points in Options Day Trading

This options day trading strategy is especially beneficial in the Forex market. It refers to the act of pivoting or reserving after a support or resistance level at the market price has been reached. It works in the same way that support and resistance breakouts do.The following are typical strategies for this options day trading style:

If the support level is approaching, buy the position and place a stop just below it.

If the resistance level is approached, sell the position and place a stop just below it.

The day trader will analyze the highs and lows of the previous day's trading as well as the closing prices of the previous day to determine the pivot point. This is calculated using the following formula: Pivot Point = (High + Low + Close)/3The pivot point can also be used to calculate the support and resistance levels. The following are the formulas for the first support and resistance levels:

(2 x Pivot Point)–High=First Level of Support

2 x Pivot Point – Low = First Resistance Level

The following formulas are used to calculate the second support and resistance levels:

(First Resistance Level – First Support Level) Pivot Point = Second Support Level

(First Resistance Level – First Support Level) + Pivot Point = Second Resistance Level

When the pivot point is between the first support and resistance levels, the options trading range is most profitable.With his trading style, the options day trader is vulnerable to sudden price movements. If not managed properly, this can lead to significant losses. The options day trader can use stops to marginalize losses to limit losses with this strategy.

When a day trader takes a short position, this is typically placed just above the most recent high price close. This is placed just below the day trader's most recent low when he took a long position. To be doubly safe, the options day trader can also place two stops, such as placing a stop loss at the end of the tradea physical stop at the maximum amount of capital that he or she can afford to part with, and another where an exit strategy is implemented.

CHAPTER 5

Avoidable Pitfalls

All successful options traders go through a learning curve before they can consistently profit. Some of them make a concerted effort to learn by spending countless hours reading about the subject or by attending seminars.

viewing video tutorials Others learn at a slower pace, and once they've mastered the fundamentals, they lean more toward learning from their own experience. Regardless of your learning style, one way to shorten your learning curve is to learn from the mistakes of others.This section outlines six of the most common mistakes made by inexperienced traders, all of which are easily avoidable.

Purchasing Naked Options with No Hedging

This is one of the most common mistakes made by inexperienced options traders, and it is also one of the most costly, potentially bankrupting them in no time.Buying naked options entails purchasing options without any protective trades to protect your investment if the underlying security moves against your expectations, resulting in a loss on your trade.

Here's a Good Example:

A trader believes a particular stock will rise in the short term and believes he can make a large profit by purchasing a few call options, so he makes the purchase. The trader understands that if the underlying stock's price rises as expected, the potential upside on profits is limitless, whereas if it falls, the maximum loss is limited to the amount invested in purchasing the call options.In theory, the trader's assumption is correct, and this one trade may pay off. However, it is equally possible that the stock will not move as expected, and may even fall. If the latter occurs, the call option prices will begin to fall rapidly and may never recover, resulting in significant losses for that trader.It is nearly impossible to predict a stock's short-term movement accurately every time, and the trader who consistently buys naked options in the hope of getting lucky is far more likely to lose much more than he or she gains in the long run.

The following conditions must be met for a person to profit after purchasing a naked option:

The trader must correctly predict the direction of the underlying stock's movement.

The directional movement of the stock price should be swift enough to allow the position to be closed before its gains are eroded by time-decay.

The increase in the premium price of the option should also compensate for any potential drop in implied volatility since the option was purchased.

The trader should exit the trade at the appropriate time before the stock's movement reverses.Needless to say, expecting everything to fall into place at the same time is unrealistic, which is why naked-options traders frequently lose money even when they correctly predict the direction of the underlying stock's movement.

Having said that, many such traders frequently believe they will fare better the following time after a botched trade and rinse and repeat their actions until they have lost most of their capital and are forced to quit trading altogether.My advice to you is to never buy naked options (unless they are part of a larger strategy to hedge a position) because the risk is simply not worth it.Nota bene: Unlike buying naked options, which have a finite risk limited to the price of the premium paid, selling naked options has unlimited risk and must be done with extreme caution.Avoided as well unless properly hedged.

Overestimation of Time-Decay

A second common blunder made by inexperienced traders is underestimating time decay.If you are a buyer of an option and don't get a chance to exit your trade quickly enough, time-decay is your worst enemy.If you are a call option buyer, you will notice that even when the price of your underlying stock rises every day, the price of your call option does not rise or even falls. Alternatively, if you are a put option buyer, you may notice that the price of your put option does not increase despite a fall in the price of the underlying stock. Both of these scenarios can be perplexing to someone new to options trading.

The aforementioned issues arise when the rate of increase/decrease in the underlying stock's price is insufficient to outstrip the rate at which the option's time value is eroding daily.To ensure a profitable trade, any trading strategy employed by an options trader should ideally have a method of countering/minimizing the effect of time-decay, or should make time-decay work in its favor.

Investing in Options with a High Implied Volatility

Another common blunder is purchasing options during periods of high volatility.Option premiums can become ridiculously overpriced during times of high volatility, and if an options trader buys options during such times, even if the stock moves sharply in line with the trader's expectation, a large drop in implied volatility would result in the option prices falling by a fair amount, resulting in losses to the buyer.A specific circumstance I recall what happened the day the 'Brexit' referendum results were announced. The Nifty index, like most other global indices such as the Nasdaq 100, fell sharply as a result, while the volatility index (VIX) increased by more than 30%. That day, the options premium for all Nifty options had skyrocketed. However, this increase in volatility was caused solely by the market's knee-jerk reaction.

As a result of an unexpected result just a few days earlier, the market stabilized and began to rise again; the VIX fell sharply, lowering option premium prices accordingly.Options traders who bought options when the VIX was high would have realized their mistake a day or two earlier when the option prices fell, causing them significant losses as the volatility began to return to normal levels.

Time is not being wasted.On Wall Street, there is a well-known saying: "Cut your losses short and let your winners run."

Even the most seasoned options traders will make a bad trade now and then. What distinguishes them from novice is that they understand when to concede defeat and cut their losses. Amateurs hang on to losing trades in the hope that they will recover, only to lose a larger portion of their capital. Experienced traders, who understand when to admit defeat, exit early and reinvest the capital elsewhere.

It is critical to cut losses as soon as possible, especially when trading a directional strategy and making a bad call. The prudent course of action is to exit a losing position if it moves against expectations and erodes more than 2-3% of your total capital.

If you only use spread-based strategies, your losses will always be far more limited whenever you make a bad call. Regardless of strategy, when it becomes clear that the probability of profiting from trade is too low for whatever reason, it is prudent to cut losses and reinvest in a different position with a higher chance of success rather than simply crossing your fingers or appealing to a higher power.

Putting Too Many Eggs in One Basket

The experienced hands are always aware that they will occasionally lose a trade. They also understand that they should never bet too much on a single trade, as this could significantly erode their capital if it goes wrong.

For this reason, professionals spread their risk across multiple trades and keep a maximum exposure of no more than 4-5 percent of their total available capital in a single trade.As a result, if you have a total capital of $10,000, do not engage in any single trade that could result in a loss of more than $500 in the worst-case scenario. Following such a practice will ensure that the occasional loss can be absorbed without seriously depleting your cash reserve. If you do not follow this rule, you may have the misfortune of having many months' worth of profits wiped out by a single losing trade.

Using Brokers Who Charge Exorbitant Fees

Saving a penny equals earning a penny!

I didn't pay much attention to the brokerage I was paying when I first started investing in stocks many years ago. After all, the trading services I received were provided by one of the country's largest and most reputable banks, and the brokerage charged by my provider was not significantly different from that of other banks that provided similar services.

Many discount brokerage firms began to flourish over the years, charging significantly less, but I had not bothered changing my broker because I was used to the old one.It wasn't until I calculated the differences that I realized having a low-cost broker made a significant difference.

If you trade in the Indian stock markets, the table below provides a quantified breakdown of how brokerage charges can eat into your earnings over a year if you choose the wrong broker. In the table below, the regular broker is the bank whose trading services I previously used, and the discount broker is the one I now use. For the record, the former is also India's third-largest private-sector bank, and the latter is the country's most reputable discount brokerage firm.

The table above clearly shows that using a low-cost broker makes a significant difference, especially when trading a strategy like the Iron Condor (a relatively low-yield but high-probability strategy).Furthermore, it is not just the brokerage fee that burns a hole in your pocket; the annual maintenance fee for a regular broker is also higher, and all of these costs will make a significant difference in the long run.

Regardless of where you trade, always choose a broker who offers the lowest possible brokerage because it will make a difference in the long run. Make a quantitative comparison using a table (similar to the one I used above), and it will be easier to decide who to go with.Note for Indian Traders: If you are a trader based in India or trade in the Indian stock markets, I strongly recommend using Zerodha, which has consistently been rated the best discount broker in the country. I've been using their services for a few years and have found them to be especially good. Their brokerage rates are among the best in the country, and they also offer excellent support when needed, as well as an extensive knowledge base of articles. Finally, their trading portal is very user-friendly, so placing an order is quick and easy.

CHAPTER 6

Optional Understanding

The big question is, how do you put your skills to use to make money on the stock market? You must be able to recognize patterns and setups as they appear. This is followed by a possible method of application. Rules are made. Charts depict patterns as well as the locations where the rules forIdentifying entry and exit points should be used.

Based on the last increase or break, determine whether the congestion is a re-accumulation or a re-distribution. Assume this until you see a congestion pattern that tells you otherwise.

The halt

We propose two steps: an average spread lower than the last reaction low or the span of the entry bar lower than the entry bar. The stop will be tightened once we have some movement. If the price does not behave properly within three bars, close the position. Then do not wait until the stop button is pressed.

Should you trade or not?

If you are not invested in the market, you are not putting your money at risk. This trading style restricts exposure to approximately 10% to 15% of the total observation period. You are not in the market between 85 and 90 percent of the time. A position can be held during an accumulation or distribution phase. Although there is nothing wrong with this approach, it does expose you to the risk of losing a significant portion of your profits. The pattern may be one of distribution rather than accumulation. You'll need to study a lot of charts until you find one that works for you and fits your trading style. This method necessitates a great deal of deliberation. To reduce uncertainty, they should try to automate as many rules as possible.

Exchange High-Value Assets

Active trading is best suited for stocks and/or futures that are moving or in trend phases, rather than boring securities that are constantly going sideways. The definition of a moving value is highly subjective. Many sources cite lists of securities that outperform and outperform others, and Investor's Business Daily is one of the best.

The following characteristics can be found in moving securities: Volatility has increased.

Securities in the rising phase have reached a new four-week high.

Significantly slanted upwards or downwards in the last 20 days sliding average

The top values in a particular market segment

Brief Synopsis

Remember that the goal of this game is to win, not to be in 90% of all price moves. Open positions when certain patterns appear and profit when the target price is reached or the first indication that the offer exceeds demand.

These fundamental principles apply to all-time horizons, including day trading. Use weekly charts if you are looking for the long term. This will result in many false signals, but there are stops. You will only make money by studying countless charts and drawing your entry, exit, and stop-loss points. As a result, you internalize and adopt these approaches. After that, you may be able to succeed in trading. One of the most difficult aspects of trading is closing a position near the end of an outbreak or during a buying surge. Simply tell yourself that you are a nice person: everyone wants the stock, and you give it to them.

The General Motors study could be one example of how to design a supply-demand-based trade system. Make two charts: one that shows what you should have done and one that shows what you did. Learn through comparison. Recognize the forces that act at critical junctures.

Elliott Wave Theory: A Practical Application

Many traders are perplexed by the Elliott Wave Theory. We won't get into the ambiguity of this theory, but we will apply it to a trading strategy that should prove successful. This is one of the best Cycle theories because it allows for non-harmonic movements.

There are numerous approaches to trading securities. These are broadly classified as fundamental and technical approaches. Some technicians prefer to combine both methods for the best market approach. Bushels, hectares, consumption units, revenues, book values, and so on are all part of the basic access. Technical analysis looks at past price movements to forecast future ones. Elliott published a series of articles describing the Elliott wave principle in 1939. The Elliott Wave Theory is one of the best technical methods for market analysis, and anyone with a serious interest should include it in their studies.

Is it possible to predict price trends using Elliott Wave Theory and profit from this knowledge? If the theory is not made into an exact science, the answer is a cautious yes. Elliott Wave Theory allows for both harmonic and non-harmonic course movements. The majority of cycle theories employ principles based on harmonic movements. It becomes difficult as soon as nonharmonic movements occur.

The following Elliott Wave Theory summary condenses the ideas into a manageable size:

Ascending moves are made up of five waves, with two of them being corrections. Falling movements are ineffective. The odd waves travel in the opposite direction of the main motion. Straight waves run in the opposite direction of the main current. Shaft 2 is corrective. 1. shaft Shaft 5 replaces Shaft 4. There are sometimes nine or more waves. Elliott solves this issue by referring to these movements as extensions.

Shaft 4's endpoint is higher than Shaft 1's height. Elliott specifies length proportions precisely, such as shaft 4 being shorter than waves 3 and 5. However, it has been discovered that this is not always the case.The movements are divided into one-degree-smaller waves. What exactly does "one degree lower" mean? This is a difficult question to answer, which is one of the reasons why applying the theory is so difficult. One suggestion is to look for it in the next few weeks. Look for the smaller grade on a 30-minute chart if you have a daily chart. The following smaller degree also requires five waves to complete the higher-order wave 1 and is thus identical to the daily chart.

Corrections in Three Dimensions

After a thrust, triangular corrections consist of a five-point pattern (ABCDE). The nature and location of such a pattern frequently allow conclusions to be drawn as to whether or not a turnaround is imminent.

A-Shape Modifications

The length and duration of the first correction wave or A-shaped correction of the thrust are critical in determining the overall course of the correction and the likelihood of a turnaround.

Look for the use of the A-wave (the first correction wave to rise) to determine the type of correction and the likely direction of the price after the correction has ended. Then you can see four different price movements. If the A correction wave's extent is the same, the following should be deduced:A single correction wave is indicated by a percentage of 25% to 35%. A three-wave correction is indicated by a percentage of 35% to 50%. 50% - 75%: This indicates a five-wave correction.More than 75%: mostly a possible trend reversal.

Predictions for Corrections

This type of price development may result in a reversal. Here are the supply and demand forces at work. A reaction 75 percent of the way from the starting point makes a clearer statement than a reaction 25 percent of the way from the starting point.

Understanding the Terminology of Options

The duration of the option is a consideration for logical reasons. If you want to control an asset for five years rather than one year, the cost of doing so will be higher. If you only need the asset controlled for one day, it will be less expensive.This is because the more tightly an asset is controlled, the more likely it is that something (there's that word again) will occur to affect its price. If, for example, the property was only under your control for one day, it is unlikely that a major real estate transaction involving your property will be reported on that day.

CHAPTER 7

Choosing Stocks

Avoid penny stocks at all costs.People enjoy trading in penny stocks because they are inexpensive and can provide significant momentum. These two characteristics make them a favorite of most small-budget traders. These, however, areBecause of these characteristics, every trader should avoid penny stocks. It's difficult to predict which way the stock will move, and most of the companies in which penny stocks trade are

shady.As a beginner, your primary focus should be on trading in solid stocks with a proven track record of performance. As a result, no matter who may try to sell them to you, avoid penny stocks.

Look for the following characteristics:

Liquidity

Many things in the market can make a trader's life difficult, and poor liquidity is easily at the top of the list. The volume or number of shares traded in a day is referred to as stock liquidity. If a stock has low liquidity, it will be difficult to sell or square off your position in that stock.

Stocks with little liquidity are also simple to manipulate. Even a small number of large traders can generate phony momentum in such stocks, and you may fall into this trap.

A wider spread is another major issue with low liquidity stocks. The spread between the bid and ask prices is so wide that most traders are unable to close their positions profitably/At first, you should only invest in stocks that have high liquidity.

Take note of the volatility.Volatility in the stock market is not necessarily a bad thing. A certain level of volatility is desirable in good stocks so that you can make money trading them round-trip in a single session. However, if the market as a whole is highly volatile, or if a specific stock has become highly volatile due to certain news, result declarations, litigation, or any other positive or negative information, you should avoid trading in that stock. Certain strategies can assist you in making money through options trading, but trading can be extremely risky when a stock is highly volatile.

The majority of the action in a highly volatile stock occurs within a few minutes, and by the time most day traders enter the stock, it has begun to move in the opposite direction. As a result, it is preferable to avoid such chaos and wait for the market to calm down before entering a trade. As a beginner, your primary focus should be on making normal trades in a normal market.

Stocks with a High Correlation

Even though the stock market is fraught with uncertainty, every trader prefers to rely on dependable stocks. Stocks that do not fluctuate erratically have a better scope for a day trader because mapping them becomes easier. Correlative stocks are so named because they have a strong correlation with the movement of specific sectors, indices, and segments.As a new trader, you should concentrate on stocks that are not overly volatile. You may not notice any abrupt or erratic movements in them, but this will save you from several unpleasant surprises.

Stocks That React to Market Trends

We've always been taught to stand out and swim against the current. We've been told that the winners don't follow the league; instead, they create their own. Well, in the stock market, you wouldn't want to bet on such winners, to begin with.Such stocks can provide an excellent starting point, but there is no way in the world that you can predict them. They are rocky and dangerous.

It is always preferable to find stocks that follow the market trend. This simply means that you should look for stocks that are outperforming the market. IfWhen the market is up, these stocks will rise along with it. If market sentiment is bearish, it will exhibit a downward trend. Such stocks will provide you with the opportunity to profit during both bull and bear markets.

The majority of stable stocks exhibit such movements. You can rely on them, and taking a position and exiting it on the same day is relatively simple in such stocks. You wouldn't want to invest in a rising stock when the market is falling, only to find that once you do, the movement stops or reverses. Such stocks are extremely dangerous, and there are a lot of them around. Sticking with the big and dependable ones can help you avoid such problems.

Fundamentals that work

Although many experts would argue that fundamental analysis has no place in day trading, don't believe them completely. Only these types of stocks survive when the market is in a slump. The reason is simple: when the tide is out, traders prefer to stick to safer bets.

Fundamentally sound stocks will always be more dependable. The market believes in them. Even minor news about their profits and expansion can cause significant movement in such stocks. Even with big news, you might not see such movement in smaller stocks because most traders don't trust them.Initially, only trade stocks with strong fundamentals. They will assist you in understanding how the market works, and once you feel ready, you can begin experimenting with others.

Pattern of Ownership

This is another critical point that is frequently overlooked. Stocks are owned by both retail investors and traders like you and me, as well as institutional investors. Both types of investors have distinct purchasing and selling habits.

A retail investor can sell all of his or her held shares at the drop of a hat. When bad news arrives, retail investors are among the first to flee. However, institutional investors are unable to do so. They manage very large portfolios, and their decision-makers require approval at multiple levels. This means that a stock in which institutional investors have a significant stake will be more reliable because it will have a high level of volatility even after a correction.

significant news event The slow response of institutional investors also ensures that there is no sudden panic or crisis-like situation because a large number of stocks are locked with them.Looking at stock ownership patterns can help you understand the risk associated with the stock. There can be no definite knowledge about the people who hold a stock if it is primarily held by retail investors. It may only take a small group of people to artificially boost the stock's momentum. They can also dump all of the shares at once. That is simply not possible for institutional investors.As a new trader, invest in stocks in which institutional investors, such as mutual funds and hedge funds, have a significant stake. This type of trading will keep your risk under control.

Understandable Chart Patterns

When you start reading technical charts, you'll notice that some stocks make a lot of sense. They adhere to patterns. Their movements can be predicted to some extent. They aren't particularly choppy or jumpy. You will also come across stocks that do not follow any pattern while doing so. They have no relationship to the indices or segments. They are nomads. Such stocks are risky to trade daily.One thing that every day trader should keep in mind is that you don't want to be stuck with a stock indefinitely. Regardless of how good or bad the stock is. You want to be able to get in and out of that stock quickly. Stocks that do not follow a discernible pattern may cling to you. Once you've purchased them, understanding or predicting their movement will be difficult, and you won't be able to get out.The best way out is to look for stocks with a clear chart pattern. Stocks that move in a predictable pattern are always a better bet.

Adaptability to the New Flow

Finally, sensitivity to news flow can be a valuable asset for an intraday stock. Some stocks respond well to news events and provide an excellent trading opportunity. Some stocks, however, would remain dormantregardless of the type of news that comes in. They have thick skin and can be unpredictable when it comes to trading. Such stocks should be avoided.Look for stocks with strong movement and sensitivity to news events, as these will provide you with trading opportunities.

Excessive Volume

No matter how appealing a stock appears, if it lacks volume, it is unsuitable for intraday trading. Don't fall for such stocks because the risk of becoming entangled in them is very high. This is the first and most important quality to look for when selecting your stock of the day for trading.

Putting Support and Resistance to the Test

Look for stocks that are testing their levels of support or resistance. These stocks have the potential to break out, and you will have a great opportunity to profit from them. Examine their levels and historical patterns carefully. If they have done this in the past, it is a good sign.

Low or high for the previous 52 weeks

Stocks that are near their 52-week low or high can also provide a good trading opportunity. Such traders can make a breakout and set new targets, and if you can correlate that with the fundamentals of these stocks, you can create a trading opportunity.

Week's Winners and Losers

Because these stocks will be in the news, trading in them may be a good idea. However, you must exercise caution because a stock that has been steadily rising for some time cannot continue to do so. As consolidation and profit booking can occur, you'll need to research whether the stock is already overbought or underbought. While considering these factors, you should also consider whether the stock is undervalued or overvalued, as this will have an impact on its escalation and fall.

Stocks with a High Market Expectation

These are the headline-makers, and they would be riding a wave. Their movements are difficult to predict because they are influenced by factors other than the fundamentals and technicalsaspects; they are based on market sentiments In any case, these stocks can provide you with short-term trading opportunities. However, keep in mind that getting in and out of such stocks quickly is always the best option. Do not try to hold your position for too long, as they can take a sharp turn on any side and lock you in.

From Your Specialization

Finally, choose stocks from your industry. As a new trader, having an open field is always preferable. However, as you gain experience in the stock market, you will realize that having a niche is always a better and more dependable option. Look for all of these qualities in your field's stocks, and you'll have very few worries.

CHAPTER 8

How Are Prices Determined

As an investor, you should have a thorough understanding of the various factors that influence the value of options before diving into the world of options trading. Among the factors are the

intrinsic value, current stock price, expiration date, interest rates, volatility, and paid cash dividends You may come across various options pricing models that use all of these parameters to determine the market's option fair value. In many ways, options trading is similar to any other type of investment; all you need to do is understand all of the factors that are used to price them.

Let's start with the most important drivers of option prices: the current stock price, intrinsic value, volatility, and expiration time. The stock's current price is somewhat obvious. The movement of the stock price up or down has an immediate, but not equal, impact on the option price. When the price of a stock rises, the price of a call option rises as well, while the price of a put option falls.When the stock price falls, the price of puts and calls falls in the opposite direction.

Intrinsic Worth

It is the value that any option would have if it were exercised right now. In layman's terms, intrinsic value is the total amount by which an option strike price is in the money. It is also the portion of an option's price that is not lost when time appears to be running out or when the expiration time approaches. Calculating the intrinsic value of any call or put option is simple and can be done as follows:

The intrinsic value of a call option is equal to USC – CS, where USC is the current price of the underlying stock and CS is the call strike price.The intrinsic option value can directly reflect the effective nature of the financial advantage that can be obtained if the relevant option is exercised immediately. In layman's terms, it's the bare minimum of an option's value. Options that trade out of the money or at the money have no intrinsic value.

The intrinsic value of a put option = PS – USC, where PS is the put strike price and USC is the current price of the underlying stock.

Assume Elegant Electric (EE) stock is selling at $35 per share. The intrinsic value of the EE 20 call option would be $15 ($35-$20 =

$15) because the option holder can easily exercise the option to buy shares of EE at $20, turn around, and automatically sell them in the market for $35 and profit $15.

The Time Value

The extrinsic value, also known as the time value, is the total amount by which the option price exceeds the intrinsic option value. It is directly related to the total amount of time that any option has until it expires. The formula for calculating the time value of options is simple:

Time value = Option price – Intrinsic value

The more time an option has until its expiration date, the more likely it will be profitable. The element of time.Any option's value tends to decay exponentially. The derivative of the option time value is a complicated equation. As a general rule, an option will lose one-third of its value during the first half of its life and two-thirds during the second half. This is a critical consideration for security investors because the closer the expiration date, the more movement in the underlying asset price is required to impact the option price.

Option time value is also affected by market volatility. The time value of the option will be very low for stocks that are not expected to move much. The time value of the option will be low for all stocks that are not expected to move significantly. The converse is true for more volatile stocks.

Volatility

Most of the time, quantifying the overall effect of volatility is difficult and subjective. Today, various types of calculators are available for calculating estimated volatility. When dealing with options trading, you are likely to encounter several types of volatility. HV, or historical volatility, aids in predicting the magnitude of any underlying stock's future movements. Two-thirds of all possible occurrences of a stock's price will occur within one standard deviation of the stock's one single standard deviation move over a fixed period. HV is used to depict the volatility of any market.

Implied volatility is calculated using current market prices and is frequently used in theoretical models. It is extremely useful in determining the current price of any existing option. It also assists option players in properly assessing trade potential. For an options trader, implied volatility is used to forecast future volatility. In layman's terms, it can reflect the current mood of the options market. This sentiment will then be reflected directly in the options price, assisting traders in assessing future option volatility as well as stock volatility based solely on option prices.Any stock investor who is serious about using options to capture the potential nature of movement in a specific stock must first understand the overall process of how options are priced. Having proper knowledge of current and expected volatility in option prices is also required for any type of investor who wishes to fully capitalize on stock price movement, up or down.

CHAPTER 9

Markets are volatile

While the stock market has long-term trends on which investors can rely reasonably well as the years and decades pass; however, the stock market is highly volatile in the short term. That is what we mean when we say.Prices are fluctuating up and down in a short time. Long-term investors are unconcerned about volatility. This is why advocates of conservative investment strategies will advise buyers to use dollar-cost averaging. This works by averaging out the market's volatility. You won't make the mistake of buying stocks when the price is a little higher than it should be because you'll average it out by buying shares when the price is a little lower than it should be.In some ways, the stock market can be thought of as a chaotic system in the short term. So, unless there is something specific on offer, such as Apple introducing a new gadget that investors believe will be a big hit, you can't be sure what the stock price will be tomorrow or the day after that. A one-day increase does not guarantee that more will follow; it could be followed by a significant drop the next day.For example, at the time of writing, Apple's stock price had dropped to $196 on the previous Friday. It went up and down several times over the next few days, and the most recent close was $203. Short-term movements appear to be random, and to some extent, they are. Only in the long run will we be able to see Apple's true intentions.

Of course, Apple is nearing the end of a ten-year run that began with the release of the iPhone and iPad. It's a safe bet that, while it's a good long-term investment, the stock won't be moving much shortlysufficient for making good profits from call option trades in the short term (not to mention the per-share price is relatively high).Volatility is a friend of the trader who buys call options. But it's a friend to be wary of because volatility can benefit you while also getting you into big trouble.

Stocks with higher volatility are a friend of the options trader because the options trader is, in part, playing a probability game. In other words, you're looking for stocks that have a good chance of outperforming the strike price you need to profit. A volatile stock with large movements is more likely to not only pass your strike price but to do so in such a way that it far exceeds your strike price, allowing you to profit significantly.

Of course, there is the possibility that the stock price will plummet unexpectedly. That is why caution should be part of your trader's toolkit. A stock with a high level of volatility is just as likely to drop suddenly as it is to pass right through your strike price.Furthermore, while you are a beginner and maybe caught off guard, volatile stocks will attract experienced options traders. This means that when it comes to options contracts, the stock will be in high demand. What happens when something is in high demand? The price skyrockets. In the case of call options, this means that the stock will be more expensive. You'll need to account for the higher premium when exercising your options at the right time and make sure the price is high enough above your strike price that you don't lose money.Traders examine the volatility of a given stock in the recent past, but they also consider what is known as implied volatility. This is a stock market weather forecast. It is an estimate of a stock's future price movements, and it has a significant impact on option pricing. Implied volatility is represented by the Greek symbol; implied volatility rises in bear markets and falls when investors are bullish. Implied volatility is a tool that can provide insight into the future value of options.

More volatility is a good thing for options traders. A stock with low volatility is a stable stock whose price does not fluctuate significantly over the life of a contract. So, while you might want to sell a covered call for a stock with low volatility, you probably don't want to buy one if you're buying call options because there's a lower chance that the stock will change enough to exceed the strike price and allow you to profit on a trade. Remember that highly volatile stocks will pique the interest of options traders and command higher premiums. When selecting stocks of interest, you will need to strike a balance.

Being able to pick stocks with the right amount of volatility so that you can be certain of getting one that will earn profits on short-term trades is something that can only be learned through experience. Before investing large sums of money, you should spend some time practicing. That is, choose stocks that interest you and place your bets, but do not execute the trades. Then watch what happens to them throughout the contract. In the meantime, you can purchase safer call options and thus gain experience that will lead to more certain success down the road using this two-pronged approach.One thing that volatility implies for everyone is that forecasting the future is an impossible task. No matter how much knowledge and experience you gain, you will have some misses. The only goal is to outperform the market more often than you lose. The biggest mistake you can make is putting all of your life savings into a single stock that you believe is a sure thing, only to lose it all.

Options to Consider If Your Current Options Aren't Working

At this point, you may believe that if the underlying stock for your option does not move or take, you have no choice but to wait until the expiration date and count the money you spent on premiums as a loss. That is simply not the case. In reality, if a call option you've purchased isn't working for you, you can sell it to another trader. Of course, in the vast majority of cases, you will not make a profit if you take this approach. However, it will allow you to recoup some of your losses.You need to recoup at least some of your losses if you have invested in a large number of call options for a specific stock and it is causing you problems. Of course, the best course of action in these situations is rarely specific, especially if the contract's expiration date is relatively far in the future, implying that the stock has many chances to turn around and beat your strike price. Remember that in all bad scenarios, purchasing stock is an option; you are not required to do so. In all cases, the most significant loss is the loss of the entire premium. You should also keep the following rule in mind at all times: the greater the time value of an option, the higher the price you can sell the option for. If there isn't much time value left, you'll probably have to sell the option at a loss. If there is a lot of time value, you may be able to recoup the majority of your premium losses.

Let's Take a Look at Some Specific Cases

The stock is dormant. If the stock is losing time value (as it approaches the expiration date) and does not appear to be moving in any direction, you may want to consider selling the call option to recoup some of your premium losses. The greater the time value, the less likely selling the option is a good idea. Of course, the lower the time value, the more difficult it will be to sell your option. To put it another way, you'll have to accept a lower price to sell it. There are two dangers here. The first risk is that you are overly eager to sell and do so at the first opportunity. That isn't a huge disadvantage; you'll still make some money in that case. On the other hand, it will be unsettling to sit back and watch the stock continue to rise. Having said that, this is preferable to some of the alternatives.One option is to wait too long to buy and sell the shares. You may expect and see the stock appear to reach a peak, and then become a little greedy, hoping that it will continue to rise so that you can make even more profits. But then you keep waiting, and the stock begins to fall. Perhaps you wait a little longer, hoping that it will begin to rebound and rise again, but it does not, and you are forced to buy and sell at a lower price than you could have gotten. Perhaps it's even droppingenough that you miss out on the opportunity entirely. A highly volatile stock may crash unexpectedly, leaving you with a squandered opportunity.The reality is that, like everything else in options trading, because none of us can see the future, it will be impossible to know if you are making the correct decision every time. Keep in mind that the goal of your trades is to make a profit. Don't get greedy, hoping for more riches than what you see on the screen. In other words, the goal isn't to sell at the highest possible profit margin. Nobody knows what they are because predicting the stock's peak price before the contract expires is nearly impossible.

Instead, you should concentrate on turning a reasonable profit. Before you even buy your call options, you should sit down and figure out a reasonable range of values that define your acceptable profit level ahead of time. When the stock price reaches your desired range, you exercise your options and sell the shares. You take your profit and proceed to the next trade.

That is not a guarantee that you will profit on every trade, but it is a more rules-based system that will get you into the mindset of trading based on objective facts rather than unbridled emotions.

Also, keep in mind that you can exercise the option to buy the shares and then hold them until you believe the time is right to sell. At other times, you may want to exercise your option to purchase shares and keep them in your portfolio as a long-term investment.

CHAPTER 10

Candlesticks

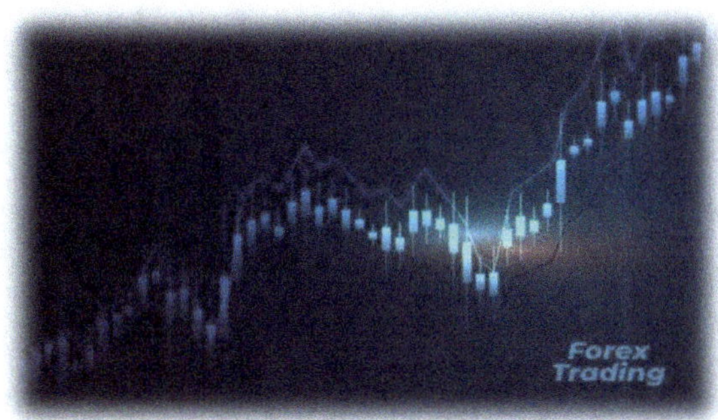

Candle outlines are a type of device that stores data for multiple periods in single value bars. This elevates them above traditional open-high, low-close (OHLC) or fundamental barslines that make a clear inference of closing costs Candles collect plans that anticipate esteem heading once wrapped up.

Consideration for Action

The characteristics of securities worth turns of events are delineated by value activity. This advancement is routinely examined in terms of esteem changes in the past. In basic terms, esteem action is a trading technique that enables a vendor to scrutinize the market and make enthusiastic trading decisions based on continuous and genuine value turns of events, rather than relying entirely on specific pointers.

The value movement trading method is vulnerable to specific assessment gadgets because it disregards the primary examination factors and focuses more on later and past value turn of events.A candle has a body as well as upper and lower shadows.

Price Action Trading Instruments

Because esteem action trading is based on previously recorded data and past worth turns of events, all specific examination instruments, for example, diagrams, design lines, esteem gatherings, high and low swings, specific degrees (of help, restriction, and blend, and so on) are taken into account by the intermediary's choice and procedure fit.The instruments and models seen by the merchant can be clear value bars, esteem gatherings, break-outs, design lines, or complex blends, for example.Candles, unsteadiness, channels, and so on.

Mental and lead interpretations and resulting exercises, as chosen by the seller, also constitute a significant portion of significant value movement trades. For example, regardless of what happens, if a stock gliding at 580 crosses the psychological level of 600 before long, the specialist may recognize a further upward move to take a long position. Various shippers may hold a contrary opinion—when 600 is reached, the person being referred to agrees with a value reversal and thus takes a short position.No two merchants will be able to disentangle a specific value movement; similarly, each will have its interpretation, detailed guidelines, and unmistakable social cognizance of it. A specific assessment circumstance (such as 15 DMA navigate 50 DMA) will, on the other hand, produce nearly identical lead and action (long situation) from various traders.Essentially, esteem movement trading is a conscious trading practice supported by specific examination instruments and recent value history, in which vendors are permitted to make their own one-of-a-kind decisions inside a given circumstance to take trading positions, based on their theoretical, lead and mental state.

Who Makes Use of Price Action Trading?

Retail handles, scholars, arbitrageurs, and despite trading firms that use shippers use esteem action trading because it is a method for managing esteem desires and speculation. In general, it will be used on a wide range of assurances, such as values, bonds, forex, items, subordinates, and so on.

Trading Actions Worth Taking

Most experienced traders who trade value movement save various decisions for observing trading models, entry and exit levels, stop-hardships, and related recognitions. Having only one framework on one (or a few) stocks may not provide enough trading opportunities. In most cases, a two-advance strategy is used:Identifying a situation: For example, a stock price entering a bull/bear stage, the channel moving, a breakout, and so on.Perceiving trading opportunities in the context: When a stock is in a Bull Run, is it more likely to overshoot or retreat? Even given the same undefined circumstance, this is an extremely enthusiastic choice that can vacillate, beginning with one shipper and then moving on to the next.

Price Action Trading's Popularity

Value movement trading is increasingly being prepared for short-to-medium term obliged advantage trades, rather than long stretch theories.

Most vendors recognize that the market is looking for a sporadic model, and there is no exact sensible way to describe a framework that will consistently work. By combining specific assessment instruments with continuous worth history to detect trade openings based on the vendor's unique understanding, esteem action trading has a significant impact on the trading system.

Focus points combine self-described approaches that provide vendors with flexibility, real nature to various asset classes, basic use with any trading programming, applications, and trading passages, and the possibility of straightforward backtesting of any perceived system on past data. Most importantly, the specialists feel in charge because the framework allows them to choose their exercises rather than erratically following a slew of standards. Finally, a plethora of theories and frameworks on esteem action trading are available, ensuring high success rates. Shippers, on the other hand, should consider the survivorship tendency, as only instances of defeating misfortune make the news. Trading has the potential to provide enticing benefits. It is the individual vendor's responsibility to obtain, test, select, pick, and follow up on what meets his requirements for the best advantage opportunities.

Patterns on Candles

A key aspect of day trading is structured by diagram designs. Flame and various charts generate a common banner that cuts through worth action "disturbance." The best models will be those that can shape the development of a profitable day trading strategy, owing to trading stocks, advanced cash, and forex sets.A Tesla candle diagram indicating value activity daily.

You will almost certainly have to choose between several trading opportunities. This is the result of a wide range of segments influencing the market. Day trading models allow you to decipher a plethora of decisions and motivations, ranging from a desire for growth and fear of setback to short-covering, stop-incident triggers, supporting, charge results, and much more.

Light models assist by painting a realistic picture and identifying trading signals and indicators of future value turn of events. While it is true that you will need to use specific assessments to succeed day trading with light and various models, it is critical to remember that utilizing them to promote your potential advantage is a more prominent measure of a gem than an inflexible science.

You will become acquainted with the power of outline plans and the theory that underpins them. This page will then show you the best way to profit from the most popular day trading strategies, such as breakouts and reversals. Your final task will be to identify the best guides to help you improve your trading style and systems.

Applied in Day Trading

Trading models, when used correctly, can be a valuable asset to your weapons store. This is because history has a penchant for repeating itself, and the budgetary markets are no exception. This emphasis can help you detect openings and anticipate potential entrapments. When you're trading, RSI, volume, as well as aiding and impediment levels, all work together with your specific examination. Regardless, stock graph models perform a fundamental function in identifying breakouts and example reversals. Acquiring the art of analyzing these models will enable you to make more astute trades and strengthen your advantages, as included in the highly regarded,' stock models for day trading,' by Barry Rudd.

Reversals and Breakouts

Breakouts and reversals are two recurring topics in the models and layouts below.

Breakout – A breakout occurs when the value surpasses a predetermined critical level on your chart. This level could be anything from a Fibonacci level to a line of support, check, or example.

Reversal – A reversal is simply a change within a valuable example. In comparison to the prevalent example, this change could be either positive or negative. You may also hear it referred to as a 'rally,'a review,' or an 'example reversal.'Inversion of a pattern. Take note of the massive bullish flame near the end of the downtrend.

On this page, you'll see how they affect various frameworks and models. You can also find express reversal and breakout methods.

Among the examples are some of the following:

The Bull Banner

Bullish banner improvements can be found in stocks that are on a strong upswing. They are called bull flags because the design resembles a standard on a post. The pole is the delayed result of a vertical climb in stock, and the flag is the result of an hour of cementing. The pennant can be a level square shape, but it is most often determined down away from the larger example. Another type is a bullish banner, in which the association appears as a balanced triangle. The state of the flag isn't as important as the hidden mind science behind the model. Essentially, despite a strong vertical assembly, the stock will not fall sharply, as bulls gobble up any offers they can get. When evaluating the length of the previous flag shaft, the breakout from a standard often results in a stunning move higher. It should be noted that these models are interchangeable and are known as bear pennants and banners. Bull standards have been exceptional throughout the most recent couple of significant stretches of 2008, however, they are starting to emerge identified with the progressing industry area rally.

Development of the Bull Banner

The amount of brain research that goes into pennant models is enormous. The cementing period serves a variety of functions.

CHAPTER 11

Market Developments

To leverage your daily investments, you must be familiar with the options market. Many day traders begin with the stock market because there are many similarities between the two markets.Stocks and options, when most people hear the term "day trading," they immediately think of stock trading. As a result, every option day trader should become acquainted with the stock market, even though the trader should never confuse the two entities. This chapter will provide you with information on the market influences that affect your success.

Choosing a Market to Trade-in

Before you enter the market in search of options to trade, you must first determine what types of assets are suitable for day trading options. Failure to do so will only leave you dazed and confused, as the market can appear to be endless. Yes, stocks are the obvious and popular choice, but they are not the only option, and they may not be the best option for you. Futures, Forex, cryptocurrency, and even corn are all viable options for day trading. Stock trading is facilitated by the buying and selling of shares in a company's portfolio, and day trading stock options means that all positions on the American stock market must be opened by 9:30 AM EST and closed by 4 PM EST. A futures market is one in which a contract is formed between a seller and a trader to buy or sell a predetermined value of the associated asset at a later date. An options day trader can profit from price fluctuations that occur during a day. The day trader must exercise caution when it comes to futures market working hours, as they can vary. As a result, the trader must be aware of when his or her position must be closed. The forex market is open 24 hours a day and is the world's largest financial market. This market facilitates the exchange of various currencies. There are many more markets to explore.When starting your options day trading career, you have many options to choose from, but it all comes down to your circumstances and the resources you have available to you. The startup fund, for example, can be a problem. This is especially common in the stock market. To participate in the stock market, a trader must have more than $20,000 in his or her trading account, whereas the forex market allows trades as low as a few hundred dollars. As a result, you can only pursue options in the stock and futures markets if you have the necessary capital.

Another factor to consider is time. Remember that some markets, such as the stock market, only operate at certain times of the day, while others operate around the clock.The strategy is also an important consideration. We'll go over this in more detail later, but some strategies work best in a specific market at specific times of the day. As a result, if a day trader excels at a specific strategy, he or she may achieve better results in specific markets.

How to Find the Best Day Trading Options

After you've decided on a market, you can narrow down the assets in which you'll look for opportunities. You must be able to identify profitable niches, and thankfully, there are systems in place to assist you in doing so. Among these tools are:

Technical Evaluation

This is the first tool we'll go over. It enables day traders to investigate market sectors to identify strengths and weaknesses. The options day trader can narrow down the options niches he or she wants to pursue within a given market by identifying those strengths and weaknesses.

There are several types of tools available for performing technical analysis, including:The Bollinger Bands are a measure of market volatility.The Intraday Momentum Index (IMI) predicts how options will perform over a single day.Open Interest (OI), which indicates the number of open options, is used to forecast option trends.Money Flow Index (MFI), which measures the flow of money into assets over a specified period.

The Relative Strength Index (RSI) allows a trader to compare profits and losses over a specific period.Put-Call Ratio (PCR), which measures the volume of put options versus call options.

Price Graphs

These tools provide a visual representation of price and volume data, allowing market trends to be determined. There are various types of charts, which are more precisely known as price charts because they show price movement over a specific period. Examples of common types include:

Line graphs

These simple charts show price movement over a set period, such as months or years. A single line connects each price data point. While the simplicity of this type of chart is its main advantage, it is also a disadvantage for day traders because it provides no information about the strength of trading during the day. The line chart also does not show the price gap. A price gap is defined as the interval between one trading period that is entirely above or completely below the previous trading period. This price cap data is essential for options day traders to make informed decisions.

Bar Chart with Open-High-Low-Close Values

This type of chart depicts price movement from highest to lowest over specific periods, such as one hour or one day. It is so named because it displays the open, high, low, and close prices for the specified period. A vertical line represents the trading range from low to high, while the horizontal line represents the trading range from low to high.A horizontal tab displays the opening and closing prices. On the chart, all four elements form one bar, and a series of these bars show movement over time.Because it provides information over 1-day trading periods as well as price gap knowledge, this type of bar chart is useful as an options day trading tool.

Candlestick Diagram

This is the type of chart that professional options day traders use. It is similar to the open-high-low-close bar chart in that price is represented on the vertical axis and time is represented on the horizontal axis. As such, it depicts the movement of prices over time.The candlestick chart's structure is made up of individual components. They are known as candlesticks, which is how the chart got its name. Every candlestick is made up of three parts. They are known as:

The body represents the open-to-close range.

The Wick: This represents the highs and lows of the day. It is also known as the shadow.

The color represents the price movement's direction. A price movement that is white or green indicates an upward price movement. A price decrease is indicated by the color red or black.Day traders can see market patterns by using the candlestick chart. Candlestick charts come in a variety of shapes and sizes.

Options Market Influencing Factors

After you've analyzed the options market and determined which options to pursue, it's time to navigate the market and place a bet on the options you've chosen.

The first thing you should do is make a trade. If you use an online broker, as most options day traders do these days, you will place your order through the digital system of the broker. When this is completed, the options day trader must decide whether to open a new position or close an existing position.

After this is completed successfully, the trade details will be electronically sent to the options day trader.Interest rates, economic trends, and market volatility are all factors that influence how the option will play out.

Summary of the Chapter

To be effective in this profession and options day trader must be familiar with the options market. The first step for a day trader is to select the market in which he or she will trade options. A stock market is a popular option, but it requires a large initial investment and has set trading hours for options

Futures and Forex markets are also popular options trading markets, with different operating times and lower initial investment amounts. These may be more suitable for some options day traders.

After determining the specific market in which the options day trader will trade options, he or she must select a specific niche within that market to trade options in. Technical analysis and price charts such as the line chart, open-high-low-close bar chart, and candlestick chart assist options day traders in determining which options to pursue.

After making this decision, the day trader will execute the options trade through the brokerage firm with which he or she works. This is usually done online, as most options day traders use digital means in this day and age. The success of this options trade is influenced by factors such as interest rates, economic trends, and market volatility.

CHAPTER 12

Options Trading StrategiesfortheDay

A successful plan would be required if you set up with a dealer and have your very own trading room ready to go. Day-trading strategies come in a variety of shapes and sizes, some simple and some complex. Before when we look at an example, we can see that there are a few critical components that will be involved in most techniques. When transacting over the internet, you can typically use charts and trends to forecast potential price changes. They are based on the fundamental theory that history repeats itself, and many wealthy traders agree wholeheartedly with that assertion.

Your map will display the most recent selling options indicators. The Put-Call Ratio Tracker, Capital Flow Index, Open Interest, Relative Strength Index, and Bollinger Bands are some examples. You'll discover that trading trends for options necessitate hard work and experience. You'd have to smooth out any creases and try a few different charts before you found one with numbers that paint a clear picture.

Options on Covered Calls

A call option is a contract option in which the holder (buyer) has the right (but not the obligation) to purchase a specified volume of a commodity at a specified price (strike price) within a specified time frame (until its expiry).If the option is exercised, the writer (seller) of the call option is obligated to sell the underlying security at the strike price. The call choice writer is compensated for taking on the risk associated with the responsibility.

Each transaction includes 100 shares, as well as stock options. If the writer of the call option owns the required amount of the security underlying it, the short call is protected. The covered call is a common options strategy that allows stockholders to generate additional income from their stockholdings acquired through the sale of call options regularly Please see our covered call strategy post for more information. Someone should purchase a bull call spread as an alternative to writing covered calls, which provides a comparable benefit opportunity but requires significantly less capital. Instead of purchasing the underlying shares of the covered call strategy, the preferred bull call spread strategy only requires the trader to purchase deep-in-the-money call options.

Because the goal of writing protected calls is to collect premiums, it makes sense to sell near-month options when time decay is at its peak. As a result, the two strategies we associate with would be selling marginally out-of-the-money call options in the near-month timeframe.

Put Options for Married Couples

Both the married put and the long call have the same limitless benefit potential, with no limit on the underlying stock price appreciation. However, the benefit is frequently lower than simply owning the stock, as a result of the cost or premium of the purchased option. When the underlying stock increases by the number of premium options received, the strategy has reached break-even. Anything above that is considered income.

The benefit of a married put is that the stock now has a floor, which reduces downside risk. The floor is the difference between the underlying stock price at the time the put was purchased and the strike price of the put. Simply put, if the underlying stock sold exactly at the strike price when the option was acquired, the strategy's loss is limited to the price paid for the opportunity.

Because it has the same profile as a long synthetic call, a married put is also known as a long synthetic call. The strategy is similar to buying a standard call option (without the underlying stock) in that both have the same dynamic: limited risk, infinite profit potential. The obvious difference between these approaches is how much less money a long call costs.

Options on a Bull Call Spread

A bull call spread is an alternative to writing covered calls that provides a comparable benefit opportunity but requires significantly less capital. Because the underlying stock of the covered call strategy is purchased, the preferred bull call spread approach only requires the trader to buy deep-in-the-money call options.If the goal of writing protected calls is to collect premiums, it makes sense to sell near-month options when time decay is at its peak. As a result, the two strategies we associate with would be selling marginally out-of-the-money call options in the near-month period. The distribution of the bull call reduces the risk of the call option, but it comes at a cost. The stock market returns are also capped, resulting in a narrow range of returns for buyers. Traders will use the bull call spread if they believe the price of a commodity will rise moderately.

This technique will almost certainly be used during times of high uncertainty.The distribution of the bull call is made up of steps that necessitate the use of two call options.Choose investments that you believe will grow in value over the next few days, weeks, or months. Purchase a call option with a strike price greater than the selling rate on a specific closing date and pay the premium. Another name is a long call with this option. Sell a call option with a higher strike price and the same expiry date as the first call option around the same time. Another term for a quick request for this option is.

Options on a Bear Put Spread

A bear put spread is a type of options strategy in which an investor or trader anticipates a moderate decline in the price of a security or asset. Bear put propagation is achieved by purchasing put options while simultaneously selling the same number of puts on the same security at the same expiry date but at a lower strike price. The potential profit with this method is the difference between the two strike prices, less the net value of the options.

An option on a note is the right to sell a specified amount of the underlying security at a specified strike price.A debit put spread or a long put spread is another name for this type of spread. A bear put spread is an options strategy used by a bearish trader to increase income while decreasing profits.A bear put spread strategy entails buying and selling puts on the same underlying asset at different strike rates on the same expiry date.A bear puts spread earns a profit as the underlying security's price falls. As a result, the net capital outlay is less than that of purchasing a single put outright. It also carries far less risk than stock shortening or protectionbecause the risk is limited to the net expense of the bear put spread In theory, selling a stock short has an infinite chance of success if the price rises. A bear put spread may be an excellent strategy unless the investor believes the underlying stock or asset will fall by a small amount between the day of settlement and the expiry date. However, if the underlying stock or security falls by more than, the dealer forfeits the right to demand the additional Benefit. Many traders are drawn to the trade-off between risk and future gain.

Options for a Protective Collar

To reduce downside risk, use the protective collar technique, which involves purchasing some protection options, selling a short call option, and purchasing a long-placed option. This strategy protects stocks from falling market values. When sold, cash-on-call options are used, and when purchased, a Put option is used.Everyone else is short on securities, and the lender must bear the risk. Long Put Options are purchased when the stock price is less than the expiry strike price. The shares are owned by the investor.Fast call option—selling the current call option until the investor believes the market price will fall below the strike price of the call option. The holder will reap the benefits. Although the buyer will not own these shares, they must buy them again if the price drops and pay the owner.

Strangle Options (Long and Short)

The endless options strangle a huge benefit, minimal risk approach that is taken while the dealer of the options considers the underlying stock and expiry date. When the underlying stock price takes a significant step either upward or downward at expiry, the long strangle option strategy generates significant returns. The profit estimation formula is as follows:

Maximum Benefit = Unlimited Benefit Gained When Underlying Price > Long Call Strike Price + Net Premium Paid OR Underlying Price — Long Put Strike Price — Net Premium Paid Income = Underlying Price — Long Call Strike Price — Net Premium Paid

One quick call with a higher trigger price and one low shot make up a medium strangle. The underlying supply and expiry date are the same for all options, but the strike rates vary. A short strangle is formed for a net credit if the underlying stock trades in a narrow range below the break-even points (or net receipt). Benefits are limited to cumulative contributions that earn fewer commissions. If stock demand rises and asset sales fall significantly, the potential liability is infinite. The full benefit efficiency is limited to earning fewer commissions overall. If the short strangle expires, the stock price trades at or below strike rates, and all options expire worthlessly, the total benefit is obtained. Because the stock price can rise indefinitely, the maximum possibility of profit loss is infinite. On the downside, there is a significant risk that the stock price will fall to zero.

CHAPTER 13

What Exactly Are Financial Leverages

Everage is a term that is commonly used in financial management. It results from borrowing capital as a means of funding and expanding investment. It will then producea few returns on risk capital It is a strategy for investing with borrowed funds. It boosts the profits of the investment. Leverage can also refer to the amount of debt that a company uses to finance its assets. When the leverage is high, it means that the investor has accumulated more debt than equity. Leverage is known to increase returns and, as a result, profit.

It multiplies the potential returns on investment. It will reduce the is likely to arise if the investment you have made does not perform as expected. The concept of leverage is used by both investors and businesses. An investor will use to ensure that the returns on his or her investment increase. The investment will be leveraged through the use of specific instruments such as margin accounts, options, and futures. Leverage will be used by businesses to finance their assets. Instead of issuing stock to raise capital, they decide to finance with debt to increase shareholder value.Investors prefer not to use leverage right away. They have the means to gain indirect access to it. They choose to invest in a company that they are aware uses force to fund and expand their investments. The company is not required to increase its expenditure. Leverage is an excellent strategy that anyone can use to multiply their purchasing power in the market. You can, however, choose to use margin to generate leverage.

Different Types of Leverages

There are various types of leverage, but they do not have to be combined with productivity. Rather than being independent, they form the entire process. They are as follows:

Leverage in Operations

Operating leverage is only concerned with a single firm's investment activities. It refers to the inclusion of a company's fixed operating costs in its income stream. The operating price can be fixed, semi-fixed, variable, or semi-variable. The fixed fee is contractual and subject to change over time. It does not have to change when the sales change, and it is expected to be paid regardless of the number of sales.

Variable costs are directly proportional to the level of sales revenue. If no sales are made during a given period, there will be no variable cost. Semi-variable and semi-fixed prices will vary in part based on the number of purchases made but will remain partially fixed. The fixed operating cost can be subject to being put into a lever, and thus investment decisions will favor using assets with a fixed price.

When a company decides to use fixed costs, it increases the impact of a change on sales when EBIT changes. The ability of a company to use its fixed operating costs to increase its earnings before interest and taxes is referred to as operating leverage. The variation in sales and profit will be the source of leverage. When the percentage of operating cost is high, the level of operating cost rises.

Leverage in Finance

When there are financial charges, there will also be financial leverage. The operating profits should have no bearing on the business costs. The sources of funds that aid in the growth of an investment can be classified. The funds may have a fixed financial cost or may not have a fixed financial cost. Debentures, preferred shares, bonds, and long-term loans all carry a fixed financial burden. It is well known that equity shares have no fixed charges at all.

The fixed financial charge is used as a lever, and as a result, business decisions will favor you when you use such funds. If there arefixed charges in a company's income stream will result in financial leverage. It is a good idea to ensure that the change in EBIT that will affect EPS will be significant. The greater the level of fixed charges, the greater the likelihood that the degree of financial leverage will increase. When fixed costs decrease, the economic advantage decreases as well.

Leverage Combined

When you combine the operating leverage and the financial leverage, you will get the combined force. It refers to the risk of not being able to cover the total amount of fixed charges when a firm can cover fully both operating and financial burdens; this is where the term combined leverage comes into play. The greater the fixed operating costs as well as the financial charges, the greater the combined force level.

Leverage of Working Capital

When the investment in a particular asset is reduced, the profit increases. This means that risks and returns are inextricably linked. When the likelihood of risk increases, the likelihood of profit increases as well. Working capital leverage refers to an individual firm's ability to increase the effect of a change in current stock on the firm's returns. It is true when the liabilities are assumed to be constant.

CHAPTER 14

Technical Evaluation

Regardless of the vehicle, you use for your actions, there are some fundamentals that you must understand. This fundamental knowledge is primarily related to market behavior. IfWhen you learn to recognize how they behave, you will be able to predict price movement more accurately, allowing you to make better trading decisions. It is worth noting that regardless of the value traded on the market, certain concepts can always apply to prices and their performance on the market.This can be explained by the fact that short-term price fluctuations are caused by independent traders and investors. We can say that the price is determined by the actions of those who invest or trade values on the market, and those prices respond similarly when similar input or stimuli are applied. Technical analysis is the study of price behavior, and understanding its fundamentals is one of the most important education points that you will need to be able to make correct financial decisions on the market.

The Fundamentals of Technical Analysis

Technical analysis is a vast subject. If you decide to enter the market and become an investor, you will almost certainly find yourself returning to study and learn something new regularly for as long as you intend to work as a trader. As a result, anyone knowledgeable in options trading would advise that a basic understanding of technical analysis is a critical step for anyone involved in the market. You do not, however, need to know everything about it right away. Because it is a broad field of study, it is acceptable if, for some aspects of your business, you only research parts of the technical analysis that are particularly relevant to that specific project. For example, consider the.Technical analysis provides over a hundred indicators for market analysis. In reality, traders typically use three or four, primarily the most popular or those with which they are already familiar.If you don't just trade options, but trade in general, you'll notice that technical analysis can be applied to any financial instrument, such as futures or stocks, for example.

We can say that their foundation is based on psychology and human nature in general, as well as how they behave in practice. We will go over some of the main topics in technical analysis to help you understand them better. These will be the topics:The foundation of technical analysis; how to chart principles and trends; patterns in technical analysis; technical analysis through the movement of averages; and technical analysis indicators.

The Basis of Technical Analysis

The term "market action" serves as the primary foundation for technical analysis. Market action represents your entire personal knowledge of the trading market, and it does not include information obtained from an insider. It is simply defined as a study that determines "how the price moves over time." It also investigates its volumes and how they change over time, if possible.

Nonetheless, the fundamental concept of technical analysis is based on the premise that market behavior is a reflection of everything that has happened and will happen with the price at a given point in time. Many factors can influence the price, and the magnitude of the impact varies depending on the market in which the trade is made. That is where technical analysis comes in; it cuts through all of those possibilities and asserts that all of the things that can be known about the price are essentially already included in the price that we see at the time we want to trade.This means that you shouldn't worry too much about the factors that influence the price, because following how the price changes over time will provide you with all of your answers. Many people initially questioned whether this kind of principle could work because it sounded so simple. If you had any doubts, the answer has already been proven, and it is yes,Technical analysis is successful, although this type of definition appears to be simple.However, one very important point emerges from all of this. Technical analysis does not guarantee price behavior. It can predict whether the price will rise or fall over a given period, but this is not always the case. It could happen or it could not. The reason for this is that, regardless of the calculation that the market must act, it is impossible to be certain that it will. The market has its ways of doing things and eventually gets what it wants. So, what technical analysis does is give you an indication of what the most likely outcome will be, which means that the only certainty you get is whether the law of probability is on your side or not.

You can do a lot of average trades and hopefully make some money, but you should never invest money or valuable goods like your house or car if you can't afford to lose it. It is not advised, especially if one successful trade has convinced you that just one is sufficient to be a good technical indicator for certain gain. This is one of the reasons why the first task of technical analysis is to increase your chances of success by analyzing prices and market behavior.

The second reason for the analysis is that prices almost always change in response to certain trends. For example, if the price rises, it will continue to rise until something prevents it from rising further. Prices, in comparison, behave similarly to Newton's motion law, which states that "a body in motion will remain in motion unless acted upon by an external force." Of course, for this to be proven, it must occur over time. The price charts depicted in many analyses would not be the way they are if this were not the case. They'd be depicted as a random movement of the prices. The third reason is that technical analysis assumes that history, as it always does, will repeat itself. If certain situations occurred in the past and are repeated in the present, the same thing will likely occur in the future as well. Because people are not expected to change in this equation, the second logical conclusion is that their outcomes will be the same as well. In a nutshell, this was the bedrock of technical analysis. Keep in mind that one of the most efficient ways to improve your trading skills and increase your chances of becoming a successful investor is to be able to use the majority of the information provided by this analysis.

There are a few counter-arguments to the use of technical analysis. Still, the only proof you need is that this analysis works and, at the very least, it can improve your chances of gaining more percentages while trading. We will, however, highlight some of the attitudes toward technical analysis:

"Charts only show what has happened in the past; how can they reveal what hasn't happened yet?" said one of the traders. The answer is simple: there is evidence from previous trades, and that evidence is used in the technical analysis under the assumption that history will repeat itself. This way, you can predict, at least with some degree of certainty, what will happen with the market price. In comparison, it works similarly to the weather forecast; if they say it will rain on TV, you know it might not rain even though they said it would, but you still bring your umbrella. The same principle applies to technical analysis, and this is how past events can be used to predict the future.

"If the prices already incorporate everything there is to know, then any price change can only come from new information that we don't yet know," said another trader. This type of concept can be found in all financial markets, not just trading options. It appears in a variety of contexts, and academics are still debating it. In contrast to popular belief among traders, this concept does not state that the current market price is correct. It simply states that it is impossible to determine whether the current price is too low or too high. As a result, the best way to deal with this concept is to demonstrate how technical analysis works in practice. In the end, if everyone agreed on this idea, we'd have no analysis and the price would always be the same. We can conclude that technical analysis has self-fulfilling properties.

This means that if the majority of traders conduct the analysis and determine that the price must rise, they will all become buyers on the market, increase in demand, and, as a result, a price rise. The same principle applies to the price that is expected to fall. This is yet another instance where technical analysis demonstrated that it works. Of course, there will always be some doubts, but does it matter why the price moved in the direction you predicted? Furthermore, if a large number of traders who are not well educated and simply want to make a quick profit fail, it can be interpreted as evidence that the idea of having a large number of traders regardless of their knowledge and dedication is flawed from the start.

How to Draw Charts of Principles and Trends

After we've seen the fundamental principles of technical analysis, we'll look at how prices are charted or graphed and what those graphs mean. There is no way around it, even if some may find it unnecessary. Throughout your trading career, you will be forced to look at this type of chart. It is easier to understand these principles if you take your time, step by step, and try to remember how they work. There are a few different types of charts, but they all use a horizontal bottom and a timescale as a vertical scale.

The price is usually to the side, and if you're just getting started, these are the only charts you should be looking at. The vertical line or timescale can be expressed in minutes, days, or even weeks, so choose the one that best suits your trading style.

However, it is not uncommon for you to be curious about what happens with the other time scales as long as they are close to the values you specified. To get a bigger picture of what's going on in the market, experienced traders look at other time scales. In this section, we will discuss three different types of charts, assuming that they all have the same time vertical line and are all in the same currency.

CHAPTER 15

Purchasing Calls

Selling covered calls is a more advanced form of training than using calls. But it's not that difficult, so let's get started.

What You're Getting

Remember that one option contract is for 100 shares, so you must be able to purchase 100 shares of the stock to exercise your right to buy.Also, keep in mind that an options contract has a time limit. If the stock price does not exceed the strike price by the deadline, you are out of luck and will lose any premium money you invested. In relative terms, the premium price will be small, so chances are you won't lose much money if you're careful and don't start by buying a large number of options contracts.

Purchasing Options Contracts is your goal.When purchasing options contracts, the goal is to purchase a stock at a lower price than its current market value. In other words, you want the stock price to be significantly higher than the strike price so that you can save a lot of money when you buy the stock. When weighing your options, consider the additional costs of the premium paid as well as commissions. Commissions can be significant in some cases, so make sure you know what they are ahead of time so you can choose a good strike price and exercise your options at the right time.

You are not an investor; you are a trader.You might be mentally programmed to think in terms of investing. An investor wants to build a diversified portfolio over time that they believe will increase in value in the long run. A trader works in the.The universe is the same, but the goals are not. You are looking for short-term profits, not long-term investments. You are not going to invest in this stock. If you wanted to keep the stock, you would simply purchase it at the current lower price. Your goal is to be able to buy at the strike price when the stock price has risen significantly and then sell it immediately to pocket the profits.Let's look at an example. Assume XYZ Corporation is currently selling at

Each share costs $30. People expect the stock to rise, and some are extremely optimistic about its short-term prospects. If you are an investor, your goal is to purchase the stock at the lowest possible price and then hold it for a long period. If you use strategies like dollar-cost averaging, you might buy a few shares every month without paying too much attention to the price on the day you buy. In any case, as an investor, you will simply purchase the shares for $30.As a trader, you're hoping to profit from XYZ's movements over the next few months. You will purchase an options contract with a premium of, say, $100.The strike price is $35 and the dividend is $0.90. The total cost of the 100 shares is $90.The stock price then skyrockets to $45. You can exercise your option to buy the shares at the strike price because it has passed the strike price. You can get them for $35 each, for a total of $3,500. But keep in mind that you are not a long-term investor. You'll sell the stock right away. You make a $1,000 profit by selling the shares for $4,500. Your profit after deducting your premium is $910. It will be slightly lower after commissions are deducted, but you get the idea. The goal of purchasing call options is to profit quickly on stocks that you believe will rise in value.

It's difficult to predict when the best time is to buy call options. You don't want to do it during a major recession. The best time is during a bull market, or when a specific company is expected to hit on something big, which will cause its market value to skyrocket. A good time to look is also after a recession has hit but before it has passed the bottom out period.

The Advantages of Purchasing Call Options

Particularly

Call options allow you to control 100 shares of stock without actually investing in them—unless they reach a price that allows you to profit.

Call options allow you to sit and wait for the market to move before making your move. If your bet fails, you will only lose a small amount of money on the contract.

In our example, if XYZ loses value and ends up at $28 per share rather than moving past your strike price of $35, you're only out of the $90 premium you paid.Call buying allows you to leverage an expensive stock.

What Should You Look for When Purchasing Call Options/Now, let's take a look at some of the things you'll be looking for when purchasing call options. You'll want to be able to buy shares of the stock you're interested in at a price lower than the price you believe it will rise to. This is necessary to ensure that the stock price exceeds the strike price. Of course, no one knows what the future holds, so this will involve some guesswork. You'll need to do a lot of reading and research to make educated guesses about where the stock will go in the coming weeks or months.

Second, when estimating the cost of the premium, you must include the cost of the premium. Assume you find a call option with a premium of $1 per share for the sake of simplicity. You'll need a strike price that is high enough to account for this. If you buy a stock at $40 per share with a $1 premium and a strike price of $41, you won't make any money unless the stock price rises above $40.$41.Remember that exercising your rights under the options contract is not a sure way to make money right away. To make a profit, you'll need to sell it as soon as possible. Of course, when to sell is a matter of judgment, as is when to exercise your right to buy. You'll want to wait until the right time comes to buy, but it's impossible to know when that time will come. This is where trading experience comes in handy, and even the most skilled professionals can make mistakes. For a beginner, the best thing to do is exercise your right to buy shares and then sell them as soon as they've reached a certain price.You've gotten far enough past the strike price to make a profit and cover the premium. If you wait too long, the stock price may begin to decline again, falling below your strike price and never exceeding it again before the contract expires.

Unresolved Interest

When you go online to look at stocks you're interested in, one of the metrics you'll notice is "Open Interest." This indicates the number of open or outstanding derivative contracts for that specific stock. This value increases by one for each option contract entered into by a buyer and seller. As a trader looking to make real money from call options, you want to look for stocks that have a large movement in the number of open trades. You'll want to keep an eye out for rising numbers. This means that other traders are interested in purchasing call options on this stock and believe it will rise in value shortly.

Of course, you'll want to proceed with caution in this situation. Simply going online and browsing random stocks is a waste of time; it could take weeks to find something.You'll want to prepare ahead of time by staying up to date on financial news. Watch Fox Business, read the Wall Street Journal, CNBC, and any other financial publ   ications that interest you. Learn about the stocks that experts are talking about and which ones the

y believe will make significant moves in the coming weeks and months. Remember that these people and experts make mistakes all the time, so you're only using it as a guideline. You also don't want to limit your search to stocks that are about to move; you should keep up with company news as well. You must keep your ears open for news such as the development of a new drug or the release of the latest electronic device.

Sometimes you'll hear about it before the stock starts attracting a lot of attention in the markets

Buying Call Options: Some Points to Consider

Don't buy a call option with a strike price you don't believe the stock can outperform.Include the premium price in your analysis at all times.Look for calls that are just about to hit the money. These are likely to generate a small profit.Call options that are out of the money may provide you with the opportunity to pay a lower premium. However, when looking to buy a call option, the premium should not be your primary consideration. In most cases, the premium will be a trivial cost compared to the money required to buy the shares and the potential profits if the stock rises above the strike price—provided, of course, that the strike price is high enough to account for the premium.Consider the time value. Longer contracts are preferable if you want to maximize your profits. Remember that with any call option, you have the right to buy the stock at the strike price at any time between now and the expiration date if the stock market price exceeds the strike price. Longer time frames increase the likelihood of this happening. Even if the price rises slightly above the strike price and then falls, with a longer time frame before the deadline, you can wait to see if it recovers. Remember, you're only out the premium if it never happens.

Begin small. Beginner traders should avoid putting all of their eggs in one basket when it comes to options. If you do that, you'll end up broke. It is preferable to begin by investing in one contract at a time and gaining experience as you go.

CHAPTER 16

Covered calls

What Exactly Is a Covered Call?

Also known as a buy-write, this is the act of selling the right to purchase a specific asset that you own at a specific price within a specified time frame, which is usually less than 12 months.

It is a two-part strategy in which someone buys a stock and then sells it on a share-by-share basis.The advantage of this type of option is that the seller benefits right away by receiving a premium payment from the holder of the option. Because the seller already owns the stock, the risk is reduced. As a result, if the stock price rises above the strike price, your costs are covered. If the trader exercises the right to purchase on or before the expiration date, you simply deliver as agreed and rip any additional benefits.

The most common asset used in this type of option is stock.If you decide to use covered calls, you must be willing to own the stock at your price even if it falls in value. Because of the volatility of financial markets, there is no guarantee that you will profit greatly from the stock you have purchased. As a result, you must be diligent in your pursuit of high-quality stocks that you are willing to own. You must be able to benefit from that ownership even if the market is experiencing a downturn.

As the seller of a covered call option, you must also be willing to part with the underlying stock if the price rises. If you have already entered into an option with a willing buyer, you cannot change your mind if the stock price rises. If the trader chooses to exercise that option, you must exercise that delivery.

The maximum potential profit from covered calls is realized if the stock price is at or above the strike price of the call at or before the expiration date. The following is the formula for this:

Maximum Potential Profit = Sum of Call Premium + (Strike Price - Stock Price)

The break-even point at the expiration date must also be considered by the seller. The following is the formula for this:

Break-Even Analysis = Stock Purchase Price - Call Premium

In addition, the seller must determine the maximum risk potential. This is equal to the stock's purchase price at the break-even point.

The seller must also be satisfied with the stocks' static rate of return and if-called rate of return. The static return is the estimated annual net profit of a covered call assuming that the stock price does not change until the option expires and option expires. The seller must know the following information to calculate this value:

The purchase price of a specific stock The option's strike price

The cost of the call

The number of days left until the option expires.

If there are any dividends, what are they, and how much are they?

The result of calculating these factors is a percentile figure. This is calculated using the following formula:

Time Factor = (Call + Dividend) / Stock Price = Static Rate of Return

The if-called return is an estimated annual net profit on a covered call assuming that the stock price is higher than the strike price by or on the expiration of the option and that the stock is sold at expiration. The same factors must be determined to calculate this figure, which is also a percentage. This is calculated using the following formula:

Time Factor = If-Called Rate of Return + (Call + Dividend) + (Strike – Stock Price) / Stock Price

The Advantages of Covered Call Options

The first advantage of covered call options is that the seller receives a premium payment, which can be kept as income regardless of whether the trader chooses to exercise the option right. Serious investors in markets that are relatively neutral or bullish can set this up as a regular cash flow. The investor can set up a regular program for selling covered calls. This has the potential to generate a monthly or quarterly income stream.The second advantage of covered calls is that they can assist investors in determining a selling price for a particular stock that is higher than the current price. Finally, covered calls have the added benefit of limiting risks because the asset protects the seller.

Risks Involved with Covered Call Options

The first significant risk of covered calls is that the seller may lose money if the stock price falls below the break-even point. This is a risk that everyone who owns stock assumes.The second risk is failing to anticipate a significant increase in the stock's price. Stocks have unlimited profit potential, but if the holder of the stock's options chooses to exercise his or her right, the seller must hand it over to this person. This can result in a huge missed opportunity because the seller now has to hand over a huge asset in the transaction.

What Is a Covered Call Option?

Buying the stock is the first step in creating a covered call. This is accomplished by buying it in lots of 100 shares. This allows you to sell one option for every 100 shares of stock you own. The advantage of purchasing stock in this manner is that you do not have to option all of them. As an example, suppose you purchased 1000 shares of stock. You can earn 5 premium payments by selling 5 contracts and leveraging 500 shares. Even if the holders of the options on those five contracts exercise their rights, you will keep 500 shares of stock.The final step is to wait for the covered call to be exercised or to expire. If the covered calls are not exercised, you are still entitled to the premium. There is always the option to buy the option back before the expiration date.The expiration date arrives, but sellers seldom follow through on this. Remember that once you option a stock, you must be willing to sell it.

How Does a Covered Call Work?

Covered calls can function in one of three ways.The stock price falls.The covered call will be worthless when it expires in this case. The bad news is that the stock price falls, but the good news is that the seller keeps the premium and thus continues to profit from the transaction. The decrease in stock price is simply the nature of owning stocks. You should have considered this before making the purchase. Remember that you must be willing to own that stock regardless of what happens, so choose wisely. However, the profit from selling the call can help offset the decrease in the stock's price.Before the expiration date, the stock price may fall. This is not a cause for concern because you are not in this position indefinitely. Although the stock price has fallen and the call value has fallen as well, this is an opportunity to buy the call back for less than you sold it for.

The stock price remains unchanged or rises slightly.This is not a lose-lose situation. While the covered call will expire worthlessly, the seller will keep the option premium. If the stock price rises slightly, even if the option holder is unlikely to exercise the right to profit from it, the seller benefits, even if the rise is minor.

The stock price rises above the strike price.If the stock price rises above the strike price before the expiration date, the option holder will exercise the right, and the seller must sell the 100 shares of stock. It's a tough pill to swallow if the stock price skyrockets, even if you've already reconciled a willingness to part with the stock, but console yourself with the fact that you make the most profit from the transaction.

CHAPTER 17

Day Trading and Swing Trading What's the Difference

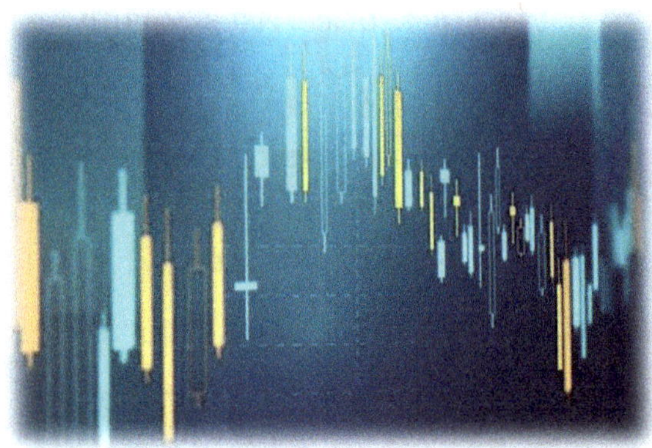

To begin, consider this fundamental question: what are you looking for like a day trader? The answer is quite simple in this case.

First, look for stocks that are following a consistent trend. Then you must exchange them all in one day. You don't have to keep them for more than a day. If you buy Amazon (AMZN) stock today, you should not hold it overnight and sell it the next day. If you hold on to your position, you are no longer day trading. This is known as swing trading.You must understand the distinction between day trading and swing trading as a day trader. The latter is a type of trading in which you hold stocks for an extended period, typically ranging from one day to several weeks. This is a different trading style, and you should not use day trading tools and strategies if you want to follow the swing trading style.Keep in mind that day trading is a business (Rule 2). Swing trading is a business as well, albeit a very different type of business. Consider owning a meat processing plant as well as a hamburger franchise.

Both businesses deal with food, but they are not the same. They use various revenue models, market segments, regulations, and time frames. Day trading should not be confused with other trading styles simply because the trades are executed in the stock market.

Day traders who are professionals close their positions before the stock market closes. Many traders engage in both swing and day trading. They are well awarethat they are running two separate businesses and are trained to manage the risks associated with these two types of trading.How stocks are chosen is one of the primary distinctions between swing trading and day trading. Many traders do not trade the same stocks day and swing. Swing traders frequently seek stocks in well-established companies that they know will not lose value in a matter of weeks.

However, for day trading, you can trade any stock, including companies that are expected to go bankrupt. Day traders are unconcerned about what happens to stocks after the market closes.

Many of the companies that you day trade are quite risky to hold overnight because they can lose a significant portion of their value in a short period.

Before you start trading, you should decide how active you want to be. How much time do I have available, and what are my current obligations? Your answers to these questions will help you decide whether you want to trade daily or buy and hold for a few days or weeks.

There are two types of active traders: day traders and swing traders. Both groups share the same goal of profiting from short-term or long-term trades. However, there are significant differences between the two that you should be aware of before deciding on your best option based on your level of technical expertise, time constraints, and personal preferences.

Day trading is essentially a type of trading in which your long or short position is entered and exited on the same day—it opens and closes within 24 hours. Day traders enter positions for a variety of reasons, including quantitative, fundamental, and technical considerations. Day traders do not gain control of their positions overnight. Swing trading, on the other hand, is a long-term investment in which the trader purchases or sells securities and holds them for days, weeks, or months. Swing traders, unlike day traders, do not intend to make trading their full-time job.

Furthermore, swing trading does not require a large amount of capital, whereas day trading adheres to the 'pattern day trader rule.' This rule governs any situation.Over five business days, a trader makes more than four trades in the same security. This trader is referred to as a "pattern day trader" because the trades account for more than 6% of the trader's total trading activity during that period. A pattern day trader must also have at least.On any given trading day, they have $25,000 in their account.

Trading during the day

Being a day trader can be extremely beneficial; however, it is not without risk. A day trader must understand that he may experience a 100 percent loss at times.Day trading, more than any other type of trading, necessitates quick and correct decisions on positions as well as estimating entry, exit, and stop-losses. The trades are quick and must be extremely precise. Day trading necessitates being present and understanding what is going on in the market at all times. Even if it does not imply that one should trade every day or consistently, the evaluations must be done regularly. This type of trading is more time-consuming than swing trading. However, it can be a rewarding all-day job.

Day trading is best suited for people who have a strong desire to trade full-time and who are disciplined, decisive, and diligent. To be a successful day trader, one must have a thorough understanding of charts and technical trading. Day trading can be stressful and intense, so traders must be able to control their emotions and remain calm in the face of adversity.

Trading in Swings

A swing trader identifies daily swings in currencies, commodities, and stocks. A swing trade, as opposed to day trading, can take weeks to complete. Swing traders are more persistent when it comes to opening trades. As the positions extend into the second day, there is the potential for enormous gains on a single trade, although there are fewer trading openings overall. Anyone with the necessary investment capital and knowledge can try their hand at swing trading.Swing trading necessitates fewer technical investigative skills and gradually focuses research and information on macroeconomics. The entry focus does not need to be as precise, and the planning isn't as important because the moves that swing traders expect to see are larger.

Swing trading does not necessitate a lot of time from the trader because frequent technical analysis and consistent sitting in front of the screen are not required. It is usually a low-stress, low-effort job. Because he is not glued to his computer screen all day, the swing trader can have a separate full-time job.

Swing traders typically need time to practice. The longer a trade is open for days or weeks, the greater the chances of profit than trading multiple times daily on the same security. Margin requirements are higher in a swing trade because positions are held overnight. When compared to day trading, which has a maximum leverage of four times the trader's capital, swing trading frequently has a leverage of two times the trader's capital.

Day traders must understand and use stop-loss and target levels to their advantage. While there is a chance that the stop order will execute at an unfavorable price, it is still preferable to constantly monitor all of your open positions.

Swing traders, like all types of traders, can lose money, and because they hold their positions for a longer period, they may lose more money than day traders.

Swing trading does not necessitate the use of cutting-edge technology. Swing trading can be done with a single computer and any necessary trading tools.

Because swing trading is typically not a full-time job, traders have other sources of income and are less likely to experience burnout as a result of stress.

When should you engage in day trading?

The following points summarise the ideal situation for you to be a day trader:

You are self-disciplined, diligent, and determined.

You are willing to make small profits daily by engaging in small trades.

If and when FINRA rules for pattern day traders and the SEC apply to you, you must meet the minimum capital requirementsyou.

You have the knowledge and expertise to make a lot of money.

You are not easily stressed, and you know how to deal with it.

You are dedicated to researching current trends and can take action at the speed of light.

You never have a dull day, and you seek excitement at all times.

When is it appropriate to engage in swing trading?

The following points summarise the ideal situation for you to be a swing trader:

You don't have a lot of technical knowledge.

You do not want to devote your entire life to trading. That is, you do not want trading to be your sole source of income.

You dislike stress and will opt for a less risky option such as day trading.

You don't want to be constantly monitoring market activity.

You are patient and can sit for weeks or months while studying market movements.

You have a full-time job and don't have time for day trading

You don't have a lot of cash to invest.

CHAPTER 18

The Fundamentals of Technical Analysis

Technical analysis, also known as chart analysis, encompasses all assessments and trading decisions that are primarily based on price development analysis. In this chapter, we will go over the fundamentals of charting.analysis.The concept is straightforward: a security rises falls or remains stable. The obvious reasons for individual security behavior can be of various types. The method for analyzing security can be just as diverse.

A fundamentally-oriented analyst examines audit firm reports, profit and loss accounts, regularly published balance sheets, management ability, dividend policy, sales, competitive situation, and production utilization. And that isn't all.He also monitors orders and communications from the Ministry of Economy and Finance, as well as price statistics and production indicators, among other things. It is a substantial amount of work that provides a wealth of discussion material.The fundamental analyst rates his security based on the foregoing and many other factors. If the security is listed at a price lower than its estimated value, he considers it a good time to buy. Assume he purchases his security because he believes it is undervalued. Assume, further, that despite the most varied arguments for rising prices, the security continues to fall.

Why is this so?

Let us look together for an explanation: The fundamental data, without a doubt, play a role in the supply and demand constellation. Undisputed!However, this constellation is influenced by a variety of other factors. Very often, they have a significant impact. You can already guess which factors will cause thecourse out of its current position/That's correct, it's investor behavior. The price is determined by investor behavior.

In our example, the stock is mostly sold by investors, and the market price reflects those investors' fears, assumptions, and moods.Even the fundamentalist's analysis of the stock exchange does not change this because the stock exchange is not logical. The moods of hundreds of thousands of people are reflected in the stock market price.

Irrational and rational moods!

A stock market price reflects the desires of investors; it defies logical analysis.Nonetheless, all of these factors culminate in a logical event: the trend.This is the price at which buyers and sellers agree to transact in the relevant security. What ultimately emerges from such a complicated process is so simple. And it is the trend that is important. The trend contains all of the information that is important to us. The trend is also said to have "pre-interpreted" all relevant information.The stock exchange market anticipates the future and bases its price on investor expectations. While the fundamental analyst is most likely still analyzing a company's current state, the technical analyst evaluates investor expectations.The fundamental analyst is probably going over the balance sheets again right now because he thinks he missed something. The stock market simplifies things significantly: it has already compiled all of the critical information that the fundamental analyst could consider.As an example, Google Share can be mentioned here. For years, fundamentally-oriented commentators have correctly pointed out Google's exorbitantly high valuation. In 2006, Google was worth more than the DAX groups BMW, Bayer, Commerzbank, Lufthansa, and Infineon combined. Even if one had very high expectations for future business development, according to fundamental evaluation criteria at the time, and evaluation beyond good and evil.

The Google IPO was already priced in the $100 range, which was deemed excessive. That didn't stop the stock from rising 375 percent in less than two years to a high of $475. Many fundamental analysts considered Google's stock to be short at $100, $200, $300, and $400. The stock price, on the other hand, continued to rise.The share has increased twelve times in less than ten years since its initial public offering. And the rally appears to have no end in sight.Should one short the stock solely on the grounds of fundamental overvaluation, i.e., sells it short? No way, no how. This is demonstrated in the following example. You would have burned your fingers almost the entire "lifetime" of the stock as a day trader. During the Internet boom at the end of the 1990s, many fundamentally-oriented market participants made the mistake of "value-shorting" and suffered a significant shipwreck. Simply because the price-moving impact of "none" fundamental factors was underestimated.So far, so good, but how does this help us in our studies?There is, however, an undeniable phenomenon. That is to say, courses change according to trends. And these tendencies tend to persist until the supply-demand constellation shifts. And there's more:

The difference in supply-demand constellations is associated with specific patterns, known as chart formations. These formations, as well as the overall trend, can be studied.

Fine!

The best part is that these analyses have always been relatively reliable. And they will continue to do so in the future because investor behavior is the only constant on the stock exchange. And this will not change because man does not change in terms of moods, hopes, doubts, or greed.So we have a suitable tool, namely the price trend in a chart, to make forecasts—pictures that can say a thousand words.

A Trend's Fundamental Concept

A trend is a price movement that runs in the same direction over a longer period in chart analysis. The primary goal of chart analysis is to filter out-trend phases to invest in them.

The concept of trend is essential for the technical approach to market analysis. And this market trend is significant because our transactions are aligned with trends.

The Trend Is Moving in Three Directions

These trends should not be interpreted as simple price movements. Trends, on the other hand, take the form of jagged movements.

These jagged movements resemble successive waves. These waves have both highs and lows. The direction in which these waves move indicates the market's trend.

In total, there are three trends: upwards, downwards, and sideways.

Let's take a closer look at some market trend examples and characteristics below.

Figure 1 depicts the patterns of an ascending and descending trend. A rising trend is defined by a series of successively higher lows and highs. A downward trend is the inverse of an upward trend.

1st Figure

This has a distinct pattern of lower highs and lower lows. As you can see, describing an upward or downward trend is simple. What is left is the sideways trend depicted in Figure 2. A sideways trend is defined by a series of equally spaced highs and lows.

2nd Figure

Many investors believe that a market can only go up or down. However, it frequently moves sideways in these so-called trading ranges, with upward and downward trends interrupting it. The peculiarity of such sideways trends is that supply and demand are balanced. Such market phases are also referred to as trendless, which is not entirely accurate but is commonly used.Examine the three trend directions again: upwards, downwards, and sideways. It is easy to believe that we should buy in uptrends; after all, we expect a trend to continue until it reverses. As a result, in downtrends, we should sell short and do nothing in sideways trends.

A Trend's Three Classifications

A trend is classified once more, in addition to the three possible directions. These categories divide trends into three types: long-term, medium-term, and short-term.

Long-term trends, also known as primary trends, last more than a year. Primary trends are not straight, but rather consist of upward movements and corrections (in the case of an upward trend). These upswings and corrections are medium-term trends, also known as secondary trends. They can last anywhere from three weeks to a few months. Figure 3 depicts the primary and secondary trend scheme. Figure 3 depicts a longer-term upward movement and a longer-term downward movement.

3rd Figure

Longer-term upward and downward movements are made up of three medium-term upward and downward movements, each of which is broken up by two corrections. These figures do not always have to be correct, but they should be used as a guide.A primary trend's direction must be understood. This is because rallies are strong in these long-term upward movements, while reactions, i.e., corrections, are weak. Long-term downward movements are different in that the reactions (corrections) are strong, whereas rallies are also strong, but short-lived and sometimes difficult to predict. If you understand the long-term trend, you will be better prepared to understand the nature of the medium-term rallies and corrections.

Short-term trends can be deduced from medium-term trends. Short-term trends are also known as tertiary trends. They have a much shorter "expiration date" and typically last no more than two to three weeks.Now that the trends have been classified, a few critical points must be made.Purchases are appropriate for an investor when the primary trend is just beginning to turn up. When the primary trend is in its early stages of decline, the investor should liquidate.As a trader, you should position yourself in a long-term upward trend so that you can buy the start of medium-term upward movements.

The medium-term trend is especially important in our classification.It is used in the majority of trend-following positioning approaches.The reversal of a tertiary downward trend into a secondary upward trend would be used to make purchases.So you're moving in the direction of the primary trend and benefiting from the long-term upward trend. This is yet another reason why the trend is on your side.Trading in long-term downtrends is more difficult.You should also act in the direction of the overarching primary trend, i.e., downward medium-term movements.In other words, it makes sense to short the rallies. This is easy to say, but it is often difficult for traders who have not yet experienced a bear market and are accustomed to bull markets.

There are numerous reasons for this. On the one hand, entry into medium-term upward trend reversals is not as easy for inexperienced people as it is in a long-term bull market; on the other hand, rallies occur very suddenly and in an extremely dynamic form.They can sometimes become so independent that you don't have a suitable forecasting tool to master these price movements with the very simple tools of technical analysis.Finally, it should be noted that a good trader works in both directions of the market and that a bear market is especially beneficial to him.One aspect of the temporal classification of trends should be mentioned: this classification is only an approximation.Because, in reality, there are numerous types of trend duration, such as trends that last only a few minutes to trends that last several decades, if not centuries.The described classification of a trend is frequently used by chart traders. This also makes it easier for traders to communicate with one another.If one of the chart traders mentions a tertiary trend, the other chart trader understands what is meant, which is a short-term trend lasting less than two to three weeks.

Misunderstandings are common in practice because chart traders with different analysis intervals have different perspectives on long, medium, and short-term trends. For example, one trader may consider a two-hour trend to be a primary trend, while another considers it to be a tertiary trend.

CHAPTER 19

Stock Investing Tips and Tricks

Almost everyone is looking for a shortcut that will lead them to success. It's human nature to seek out miracles that can change everything. People are concerned about the stock market.They are concerned about losing their investments. They seek out opportunities that will allow them to secure their investments and profit.Avoiding losses in stocks is a difficult task, and even experienced traders occasionally fail to achieve their objectives. The only way to achieve success is to learn more and more about stock market behavior over time.Every trader should be aware of the following professional tips and tricks for stock exchange investing: Invest in an index fund.One of the most important investing tips is to invest in an index fund rather than individual stocks. It also depends on your objectives, but investing in individual funds is not a good strategy.

If you are serious about investing in stocks, investing in an index fund in a specific sector can be a great way to build your portfolio. It also helps to concentrate on one thing at a time. When investing in an index fund, there are a few things to keep in mind. These are the expense ratio and total assets.

Concentrate on Mutual Funds

It is a well-known adage that putting all of one's eggs in one basket is always a bad idea. When purchasing stock shares, keep in mind that you should not invest in single stocks. Always look for good growth mutual funds and invest in them. This method is the most secure, but it is the most time-consuming.It appears to be tedious and time-consuming. However, many people prefer to concentrate on mutual funds. This technique helps to reduce the likelihood of losing an investment.

The Art of Market Timing

Many novices believe that there are times when selling or buying stocks can result in profits. They all lose their money in the end. Learning about market volatility is a difficult task. Timing the market, according to some experienced traders, is not a good way to dominate the stock market. You must be able to recognize market fluctuations and sell or buy stocks accordingly. There is no such thing as the best or worst time to buy or sell stock.

Set Objectives

Setting goals is always the best method that everyone should use to achieve success. People who lack goals are similar to those who are blind. Before you enter the stock market, you should first determine your investment objectives. When you create a long-term plan, you will have a better understanding of what to do and how to get there.

To Learn Trading, Follow These Five Golden Steps

Setup: A setup is a high probability pattern to watch on the chart. It also ensures that you have a good reason for considering a trade. You must keep track of them to ensure their consistency.Strategy: There has to be a way to trade the setup and a perfect plan for it that appears to be working. Beginners should always work on their strategies and dedicate time to them.Entry: The importance of entry cannot be overstated. If you enter the market correctly, you will make a profit. On the other hand, the incorrect entry will cause you to run out of money.Stop: When engaging in live trading, there should always be a point at which you come to a halt. This should all be planned ahead of time, and you should know why you're stopping.Profit Goal: When things start to go your way, you sometimes make bad decisions. Rather than being sorry later,make decisions to set a profit target.

Maintain a Balance of Investments

There are three types of investments: low risk, high risk, and moderate risk. All of these investments have advantages and disadvantages. Maintaining a healthy balance between these three risky investments can be a wise strategy. If you're just getting started, stick to low-risk investments.

As you gain experience, progress to moderate and then high-risk investments. Low-risk investments can produce small profits, but rather than losing all of your money in high-risk investments, consider low and moderate-risk investments.

Consider the Long Term

We are always looking for short-term methods that can generate large profits. But in reality, these are insignificant. As a result, always plan for the long term. Invest your time in learning how stocks behave to make more money in the long run.

Purchase Undervalued Stocks

Value stocks are those that have been established with few variations. If you want to succeed in the stock market, you must first understand stock volatility. Purchasing value stocks can significantly increase the safety and security of your investments. Consider the earning ratio and price to sales ratio when looking for value stocks.

Diversify your investments across industries.Nobody can predict the stock market's volatility. The stock market can be impacted by a sudden change in the country or even abroad. This abrupt change could be a political activity, a storm, a disaster, or anything else out of the ordinary. Diversification of investments across sectors has been shown to reduce the likelihood of losing investments.

How much risk are you willing to take?

Before you begin trading, you should decide how much risk you are willing to take. This strategy has some advantages and disadvantages. This strategy aids in the comprehension of your game plan. Whether you are investing for the long term or have made a long-term plan, you must be clear about how much risk you are willing to take.

Manage Your Emotions

Being patient is one of the most important things you can do to achieve your goals in the stock market. The stock market is regarded as one of the most volatile markets. Nobody can predict what will happen in the next minute. People lose millions of dollars in a matter of seconds.Controlling your emotions at that time is a difficult task. However, to become a mature trader, you must be able to see your pockets running out of money. With a calm mind, you can devise plans B and C to get things moving in the right direction.

View from Every Angle

Every day, experienced traders immerse themselves in learning more about stocks. This is the reason why you gain more and more experience. Always be completely aware of what you are doing when buying or selling stock shares.You must be certain of the outcomes. There must be some strategies in place to deal with the sudden uncertainty and keep you stable in the market.

Stocks should be automated.Automating your stocks is an important step toward gaining more experience in the stock market. It also aids in the development of your security and playing on the safe side. If you do not want to do it manually, Robo-Advisors are always available to help. When you make regular investments, you avoid the temptation to time the market.

Refuse to Use Leverage

Leverage simply means borrowing money to begin investing in stocks. Borrowing money can be accomplished in a variety of ways. You can, for example, borrowfrom brokerage houses, This method is used by some newcomers to the stock market to begin their stock market journey. Because of the high risks involved, they stand a good chance of failing. When you have a lot of experience with stocks, this strategy can work for you.

Select One Industry

Investing in a single industry may be a better strategy. Professional traders only invest in one industry. Investing in a single industry has numerous advantages. If you concentrate your efforts on a single industry, you will learn more in a shorter period. You will also begin to become acquainted with the industry's fluctuations.

Risk versus Return

Simply put, higher-risk investments always have the potential for large profits. Less risky investments, on the other hand, have low-profit margins. As a result, you must be clear in your game plan about how much return you are willing to have. People are prone to making rash decisions, such as pursuing high-profit margins at the expense of losing money. Instead of regretting it later, invest in a mix of high and low-risk investments.

Buy low and sell high

This is the most well-known method, and almost all traders use it. However, some people get this strategy wrong, and instead of making a profit, they end up losing money. Calculating the standard deviation of a stock is one of the most important factors to consider when purchasing it at a low price.If the stocks you want to buy have a standard deviation of 15% or less, you're good to go. It will be a better strategy if your stock standard deviation falls below 15% in a short period. There is a good chance that that specific stock will rise now.

The Last Word

Many people believe that stocks are a scam, but if you set things up correctly, they can make you more money than any other business in the world. All you need to do is avoid focusing on investing your moneyin the stock market, but you must invest time to learn the stock market. No one can ever predict the stock market with certainty.

However, as you gain more experience, you will be able to understand the behavior of stocks and learn about the fluctuations. Consider all of the above-mentioned stock market investing tips and tricks before embarking on a live trade to ensure a successful stock market journey.

CHAPTER 20

Important Trading Rules to Remember

There is more to options day trading than a style or a strategy. If that were all it took, you could simply adopt those that have been shown to work and stick with them. Yes, options day trading is possible.

Styles and strategies are important, but they are not the be-all and end-all of this profession.The options day trader himself or herself is the winning factor. You are the factor that determines whether you will win or lose in this career—only taking the time to develop your expertise, seeking guidance when necessary, and being completely dedicated allows a person to progress from a novice options day trader to an experienced one who is successful and hitting his or her target goals.

Discipline is required to develop into the options day trader you want to be. Options day trading rules can assist you in developing the necessary discipline. You will make errors. Every newcomer in any field does, and even experienced options day traders are human and, as a result, have bad days.

Knowing common mistakes can help you avoid many of them and eliminate a lot of guesswork. Having rules to follow can also help you avoid making these mistakes.

I've compiled a list of ten rules that every options day trader should be aware of. It is entirely up to you whether or not you follow them, but know that they have been shown to help beginner options day traders become winning options day traders.

The First Success Rule – Have Realistic Expectations

Unfortunately, many people who enter the options trading industry do so to make a quick buck. Trading options is not a get-rich-quick scheme. It is a reputable career that has made many people wealthy, but only because these people invested the time, effort, study, and dedication to learning and mastering the craft. Mastery does not happen overnight, and novice options day traders must be prepared for that learning curve and have the fortitude to stick with day trading options even when things get difficult.

Losses are an unavoidable part of the game. No trading style or strategy can guarantee consistent profits. The best options traders have a winning percentage of around 80% and a losing average of around 20%. As a result, an options day trader must be both a good money manager and a good risk manager. Prepare for possible losses and make every effort to minimize those losses.

The Second Success Rule – Begin Small to Grow a Large Portfolio

When you first start with day trading options, you should proceed with caution. Keep in mind that you are still learning options trading and gaining an understanding of the financial market. Even if you are eager, do not jump the gun. After you've practiced paper trading, start with smaller options positions and gradually increase your position as you learn the ins and outs ofoptions day trading. This strategy allows you to limit your losses and develop a systematic approach to entering positions.

The Third Success Rule – Know Your Limits

You may be tempted to trade as much as possible to develop a winning monthly average, but doing so will result in a losing average. Remember that every options trader must give careful thought before entering into a contract. Never overtrade and risk tying up your investment funds.The Fourth Success Rule – Be mentally, physically, and emotionally prepared every day.This is a mentally, physically, and emotionally demanding job, and you must be able to meet the demands of it. That means maintaining good health in your body, mind, and heart at all times. Make it a point to schedule time for self-care every day. This can range from as simple as reading for pleasure to having an elaborate self-care routine in place in the evenings.

If you do not keep your mind, heart, and head in good health, they are more likely to fail you. Being constantly tired, short-tempered, preoccupied, and easily distracted are all indicators that you need to buckle up and take better care of yourself.Here are a few tasks you should complete to ensure you give your best effort every day:Get the recommended amount of sleep every night. For an adult, this is between 7 and 9 hours.

Consume a well-balanced diet. To function optimally, the brain and body require adequate nutrition. Include fruits, complex carbohydrates, and vegetables in this diet, and limit your intake of processed foods.Every day, eat breakfast, lunch, and dinner. The main meals will refuel your mind and body. Eating a nutritious breakfast is especially important because it sets the tone for the rest of the day.Regular exercise is essential. Inactivity raises your risk of developing chronic diseases such as heart disease, certain cancers, and other devastating health consequences. Adding a few minutes of exercise to your daily routine not only reduces those risks but also allows your brain to function better, which is extremely beneficial for an options day trader.Alcohol should be consumed in moderation or not at all. Quit smoking.Reduce the stressors in your environment.

The Fifth Success Rule – Do Your Homework Every Day

Get up early to research the financial environment and read the news before the market opens. This enables you to create a daily options trading strategy. Pre-market preparation refers to the process of analyzing the financial climate before the market opens. It is a necessary task that must be completed every day to compete for assets and align your overall strategy with the short-term conditions of the day.Creating a pre-market checklist is a simple way to accomplish this. A pre-market checklist might include, but is not limited to:Examine the individual markets in which you frequently trade options or intend to trade options to assess support and resistance.

Checking the news to see if any market-moving events have occurred overnight.Observe what other option traders are doing to determine volume and competition.Identifying safe exits for losing positions.

Because of the seasonality of certain markets, some are affected by the day of the week, the month of the year, and so on.

The Success Rule #6 – Examine Your Daily Performance

Track your performance to see if the options day trading style and strategies you've adopted are working for you. At the most basic level, this must be done daily because you trade options daily. This will allow you to spot patterns in your profit and loss statements. This can lead to you figuring out why and how these gains and losses occurred. These decisions lead to the fine-tuning of your daily processes for maximum results. These daily performance reviews enable you to make long-term decisions about your options day trading career.

The Success Rule #7 – Do Not Be Greedy

If you are fortunate enough to receive a 100 percent return on your investment, do not be greedy and try to take advantage of the position further. You could

Have your position turn against you, and you could lose everything. When and if such a rare occurrence occurs, sell your position and take the profits.

The Success Rule #8 – Pay Attention to Volatility

Volatility in the financial market refers to the likelihood of a price change occurring over a specific period. Volatility can work in favor of or against an options day trader. It all depends on what the options day trader is trying to achieve and where he or she is currently standing.The economic climate, global events, and news reports are just a few of the external factors that influence volatility. Strangles and straddles are excellent strategies for use in volatile markets.

Volatility can be classified into several types, which are as follows:

Price volatility describes how the price of an asset rises or falls in response to supply and demand for that asset.Historical volatility is a measure of how an asset performed in the previous 12 months.Implied Volatility is a measure of how a financial asset will perform in the future.

The 9th Success Rule – Use the Greeks

The Greeks are a set of measures that indicate how sensitive an option's price is to other factors. A letter from the Greek alphabet represents each Greek. These Greeks are determined using complex formulas, but they are the system on which option pricing is based. Although these calculations can be complex, they can be completed quickly and efficiently, allowing options day traders to use them to advance their trades to the most profitable position.

The 5 Greeks Used in Options Trading Are As Follows:

Delta

This Greek term describes the price relationship between an option and its underlying asset. A change in the price of the associated asset is directly translated into a change in the price of an option by delta. Deltas for call options range from 1 to 0, while deltas for put options range from 0 to -1. A call option with a delta is an example of a delta about a call option.

If the price of the associated asset rises by $200, the price of the call option rises by $100.

Vega

This Greek represents the sensitivity of an option's price to the implied volatility of the underlying asset. The volatility of the associated asset prices has a significant impact on option prices because greater volatility implies a greater likelihood that the price of the associated asset will reach or exceed the strike price on or before the expiration date of the option.

Theta

This Greek represents the sensitivity of an option's price to time decay of the option's value. Time decay describes the rate at which the contract's value deteriorates due to the passage of time. The closer the expiration date gets, the faster time decay occurs because the window of opportunity to profit shrinks. As a result, the longer it takes to reach an option's expiration date, the more value this option has because it has a longer period to generate a profit for the trader. Because time is always a diminishing factor, the theta is a negative number. This figure becomes increasingly negative as the expiration date approaches.

Gamma

This Greek represents the rate of change of an option's delta. At its most basic level, it indicates the likelihood of an option reaching or exceeding the strike price.

Rho

This Greek is a measure of the value of an option about changes in interest rates. Longer expiration dates are more likely to be chosen.

Interest rate changes have an impact.

Rule #10 of Success – Be Flexible

Many options day traders find it difficult to experiment with trading styles and strategies with which they are unfamiliar. While the adage "don't fix it if it ain't broke" is true, you will never become more effective and efficient in this career unless you step outside of your comfort zone at least once in a while. Yes, continue to want to work, but keep in mind that there may be better alternatives.

CHAPTER 21

Advanced Options Trading Strategies

We'll see some advanced exchanging methodologies later.

The Long Straddle

During a long ride, you'll buy a put and the equivalent hidden stock at the same time. You'll also need a similar strike price and termination date. This method can be applied to an extremely volatile stock. As a result, you have the opportunity to profit regardless of how the stock performs. Before we see how this works, let's take a step back and look at how we determine whether or not an arrangement will be profitable. We're looking at it from the perspective of the buyer.

You will profit from a call option if the stock price rises above the strike price. Regardless, you should keep the premium in mind for your estimation. If you believe a stock will go higher than $54, but you're paying a $1 premium for each offer, you should invest in a well-thought-out option with a strike cost of at least $55.

In a put option, you're playing a similar game, but you're betting that the stock will fall below the strike price. As a result, in our new situation of buying a call and a put at the same strike price and expiration date, we will buy a put with a strike price of $55. We'll stick with a $1 premium for simplicity's sake.

Now you must determine the net premium, which is the sum of the premium from the call option + the premium from the put option, in this case, $2.

You can receive a benefit if one of two conditions is met:

The price of the basic stock is greater than (the strike cost of the call + the net premium). In our model, you will benefit when the fundamental stock measure is greater than $55 + $2 = $57.

Fundamental stock price (Strike cost of put – Net Premium). When the cost of the hidden stock is less than the cost of our model, you will see a benefit.

$55 minus $2 equals $53.

The most severe misfortune for a ride will occur when the contract expires with the hidden exchange at the strike cost. Overall, the two agreements expire, and you are out of the premiums paid for the two alternatives.

A long ride focuses on recouping the initial investment. They are as follows: Breakeven point is lower: Net premium – Strike cost

Strike cost + Net premium = Upper breakeven point

Remember that you purchased the two options with the same strike price and termination date.

Let's take a look at a straightforward model. In May, the stock is trading at $100 per share. The financial specialist buys a call with a strike price of $200 that expires on the third Friday of June for $200.

$100. The speculator also buys a put with a strike price of $200 that expires on the third Friday of June for $100.

The net premium is equal to $100 plus $100, for a total of $200.Assume that the stock is trading at $300 on the expiration date. The put expires as ineffective because the stock price of the fundamental is far greater than the strike price of the put. However, the financial advisor's call alternative lapses in cash with an inherent estimation of 100 x ($300 -

(200) x 10,000 = $10,000 The financial specialist has made a reduction in the premium.$9,800.Assume, however, that the stock falls in value and is trading at $50 on the expiration date. This time, the call alternative is rendered ineffective. The speculator can purchase 100 offers at $50 each for a total cost of $5,000. Currently, he can offer them the opportunity to practice the put choice at.He receives $20,000 minus $5,000 minus $200, for a total of $14,800.

This is a fictitious model, so whether the numbers are practical or not is beside the point—the fact is that the financial specialist will benefit regardless of what happens to the stock price.

Choke

The term choke refers to a ride adjustment. In this case, you should also buy a call option and a put option at the same time. However, rather than getting them at the same strike price, you get them at different strike prices. You will need to purchase some out-of-pocket alternatives for this type of system. This is used when you believe the primary stock will experience significant volatility for the time being.

A choke will provide you with a benefit if one of the following conditions is met:

The price of the hidden stock is greater than (the strike cost of the call + the Net Premium paid). or

Basic stock price (strike cost of put – net premium paid)

The strike price of the put is typically set at a lower value. One of two prospects controls the benefit:

Profit = fundamental stock price – call strike price – net premium

Profit = put strike cost – fundamental stock cost – net premium

The Bear Spread

When the fundamental stock value declines, a bear spread is advantageous. A bear spread, like the preceding methodologies, includes the simultaneous acquisition of more than one option; however, in a bear spread, you purchase two alternatives of the same kind. A call bear spread, on the other hand, entails selling a call with a low strike cost and purchasing a call with a high strike cost.

The Bull Spread

A bull spread is intended to profit when the cost of the fundamental security increases unexpectedly. A bull spread can be done with either call or put options.

Putts that are hitched

A wedded put is essentially a protection strategy, similar to the one we discussed previously. You buy a stock and a put option at the same time to protect yourself from potential losses in the stock.

Puts with a Cash Guarantee

In money secured put, you secure the potential acquisition of stock by having enough cash in your investment fund to cover the purchase. This will allow you to buy a stock at a discount if you have enough cash in your account to do so. To put it simply, you create a fixed option and set aside the funds to purchase the stock. When you make a put bet, you are bullish on the underlying stock but believe it will experience a temporary downturn.

Rolling

Rolling an exchange simply means that you are closing your current positions while opening new ones based on the same basic stock. When rolling a position, you have the option of changing the strike price, the duration of the agreement, or both. You can proceed, which intends to extend the choice's termination date.

A move up means that when you open a new agreement, you increase the strike cost. When you believe the fundamental stock's price will rise, you use a move-up on a call option. When you are exchanging put alternatives, you use a move down. Overall, you close your alternative and reopen it with the same fundamental stock, but at a lower strike cost. A higher strike value indicates that the new position will be less costly. When you move, you are going out to save time. When you roll a call, you're betting that the stock's price will rise. In this case, you're moving to an out-of-cash position. The cost of the new call will be reduced. With a put, the inverse occurs, and the cost of the new put rises.

CHAPTER 22

Techniques for Making the Most of a Bad Situation

Good options trading strategies are the major key to any kind of success that is about to unfold in any activity.

Strategies are typically outlined in a trading plan and should be strictly adhered to in any options trading transaction that is likely to be involved. Let us dive headfirst into the best options trading strategies to date.

Collars are an accessory. The collar strategy is established by purchasing several shares of the underlying stock in the market, where protective puts are purchased and call options are sold. Using this strategy, the options trader is more likely to protect his or her capital used in trading rather than the idea of gaining more money during trading. This type is considered conservative and is significantly more important in options trading. Spreads on credit. Most traders' greatest fear is a financial breakdown, it is assumed. The trader gets to sell one put and then buy another in this side of the strategy.

Calls were covered. Covered calls are a good type of strategy in which one trader sells the right for another trader to purchase his or her stock at a certain strike price and profit handsomely. However, there is a specific time when this strategy should be used, and if the buyer fails to purchase some of the stock before the expiration date, the contract becomes immediately invalid.

Put cash on the table. Cash naked put is a type of strategy in which the options trader gets to write at the money or out of the money during a specific trading activity while setting aside a specific amount of money to purchase stock.Long-term call strategy This is the most fundamental strategy in options trading, and it is also the simplest to understand. Aggressive option traders who are bullish are heavily involved in the long call strategy for options trading. This means that bullish options traders end up buying stock during trading in the hopes that it will rise soon. In the long call strategy, the reward is limitless.Strategy for short-term call options. The long call strategy is the inverse of the short call strategy. Bearish traders are extremely aggressive in the fallout of stock prices while trading in this type of strategy. They decide to sell the available call options. This move is regarded as extremely risky by experienced options traders, who believe that prices may decide to rise dramatically once more. This strongly implies that significant losses are likely to be incurred, resulting in a complete failure of your trading structure and everything involved in it.

Long-term put option strategy First and foremost, you should be content with the fact that buying a put is the inverse of buying a call. So, in this strategy, when you become bearish, that is when you should buy a put option. The put option places the trader in a position where he can sell his stock at a specific time before the expiration date. In the options trading market, this strategy exposes the trader to a minor type of risk.

It's trading time. It is shown that trading options for a longer period are more valuable than trading for a short period. The longer the trading day, the more skills and knowledge the trader is likely to be engaged in, as he or she is more likely to gain the necessary experience for good trading. For a while, mastering good trading moves provides the trader with experience and adequate skills.Strategy for bull call spreads. In this strategy, the investor buys several calls at a specific strike price and then buys the price at a much higher price. The calls all have the same expiration date and are issued by the same underlying stock. Bullish options traders are the most likely to use this strategy.The bear put strategy. This strategy entails a trader purchasing put options at a specific price and then selling them at a lower price. These options have the same expiration date and are based on the same underlying stock. This strategy is mostly used by traders who are considered bearish. As a result, there are only limited losses and gains.The iron condor during a specific trading period, the iron condor combines the bull call spread strategy and the bear put strategy. The stock's expiration dates are still similar and are for the same underlying stock. Most traders employ this strategy when the market is expected to exhibit low volatility and with the expectation of gaining a small premium. Iron condor works in both up and down markets and is thought to be economical in both up and down markets.

Put strategy for married people. To that end, the options trader purchases options for a specific amount of money and receive the same number of shares of the underlying stock. The protective put is another name for this type of strategy. This is another bearish options trading strategy.Covered put strategy with cash, In this case, one or more contracts are sold with 100 shares multiplied by the strike price amount for each contract in the options trading. Most traders employ this strategy to obtain an additional amount of premium on a specific stock they wish to purchase.

Calendar spread strategy, long or short. This is a deceptive strategy. The market stock is said to be stagnant, not moving, and waiting for the right timing until the front-month expiration date arrives.

Synthetic long arbitrage strategy. Most traders employ this strategy when attempting to profit from differences in market prices in different types of markets with the same property.

The ratio back spread strategy is a type of put spread strategy. This is a bearish options strategy in which the trader sells some put options and then buys more options on the same underlying stock with a similar expiration date and a lower price.Back spread on call ratio. In this strategy, the trader employs both long and short options positions to eliminate consistent losses and achieve large amounts of profit over a specific trading period. The essence of this strategy is to generate profits if stock prices rise and to reduce the number of risks that are likely to be involved. Bullish options traders are the most likely to use this strategy.

The long butterfly strategy This strategy consists of three parts: purchasing one put option at a specific price, selling the other two options at a lower price than the purchase price, and purchasing one put at an even lower price during a specific trading period.A quick butterfly strategy. In this strategy, a put option is sold at a much higher strike price, two puts are then purchased at a lower price than the purchase price, and a put option is later sold at a much lower strike price. In both cases, all put options have the same expiration date, and the strike prices are usually equidistant, as shown by various options trading charts. A short butterfly strategy works in the opposite direction of a long butterfly strategy.a long straddle The long straddle, also known as the buy strangle, is a strategy in which a slight pull and a slight call are purchased during a specific period before the expiration date. The significance of this strategy is that the trader has a good chance of making good profits during his or her trading time before the expiration date is reached.Straddle that is too short. In this strategy, the trader sells both calls and put options at the same price and with the same expiration date. Traders use this strategy in the hope of making large profits while taking on a variety of limited risks.Possessing positions that are already part of a portfolio. Most traders prefer to buy and sell options that already hedge existing positions. This strategy method is thought to generate good profits while also generating losses in other situations.Trade strategy for albatrosses. This strategy seeks to profit when the market is stagnant during period.a specific options trading period or a set amount of time This strategy is comparable to the short gut strategy.

Use the reverse iron condor strategy. This strategy is focused on profiting when the underlying stock in the current market dares to make some sharp market trade moves in either direction. Eventually, a limited number of risks and profits are encountered during trading.

Spread an iron butterfly. For a specific trading period, buying and holding four different options in the market at three different market prices is involved in the trading market.Strategy for shorting the bull ratio. The short bull ratio strategy is used to profit from the increased security involved in the trading market in the same way that we normally get to buy calls during a specific period.

The bull condor spread This is a strategy that is designed to return a profit if the actual price of the security decides to rise to a predicted price range during a specific trading period, affecting large chunks of profits made by the options trader and a limited number of risks involved.

Spreading put ratios is a put ratio spread strategy. During a specific options trading period, this strategy entails purchasing several put options and adding more options with different strike prices and the same type of underlying stock.Strap straddle technique. Strap straddle strategy employs one put and two calls with similar strike prices and expiration dates, as well as the same underlying stock that is normally stagnant during a specific trading period. The trader employs this strategy in the hope of earning greater profits than the standard straddle strategy during a specific trading period.Strap strangle technique. This is a bullish strategy in which more call options are purchased than put options, and a bullish inclination is then depicted in various trading charts information.Reintroduce the spread strategy. To establish a position, this back-spread strategy combines both short puts and long puts.where the ratio of losses and profits is entirely determined by the ratio of their two puts that are likely to occur in the mark.

CHAPTER 23

Selling Alternatives

You can sell covered calls against your shares if you own 100 or more shares of a particular stock. This is a common strategy used by people to profit from their shares, but there is always the risk that your shares will be called away if the option is exercised. When you don't expect the share price to rise to the strike price of the call option over the life of the option, one strategy that can be used is to sell out-of-the-money callsthe agreement.

For example, Facebook is currently trading at $190.25 per share. You can sell a $210 call for $0.64, so one option contract would net you $64 for all 100 shares. This is for a 30-day expiration date. You could also take a higher level of risk and sell a $195 call for $4.05, giving you a premium of $4.05

Each option contract costs USD 405. If you owned 500 shares, you'd get $2,025 in premiums. It's not a bad source of passive income, and all you have to do is hope that the share price remains below the strike price.

If the share price approaches the strike price, you will face a choice: risk having the option exercised if the share price rises above the strike price, or buy back the option and reduce your profits. With a few days until expiration, the option you sold could be worth $2.05, allowing you to repurchase the five options you sold, reducing your net profit to $1,000.

You could go even further, selling LEAPS. In that case, the premium paid is significantly higher. A Facebook LEAP with a $195 call expiring in 18 months has a premium of $30.58, so selling five contracts for your

500 shares could net you $15,290. Of course, there is a greater chance that the share price will rise above the strike price over the next 18 months than there is in the short term.

The one thing to remember when selling covered calls is that if the option is exercised, you could lose your shares. Keeping this in mind, you should only choose a strike price that is greater than the amount you paid for the shares. As a result, if you are forced to sell the shares, you will not incur a loss. It may be easier to deal with the loss of the shares as a result of this. So, if we had purchased our shares at $200 per share, we would not choose a strike price of $195 because that represents a potential loss, which would be given by the price we paid for the shares minus the strike price and then less the premium aid, in this case, $200 - $195 - $4.05, so we'd lose $0.95 on the trade. If you had bought the shares at a lower price, say $190 per share, the $195 strike would make sense because even if the stock price rose and the shares were called away, we would still profit by selling the shares.

Protected puts are the put counterpart to covered calls. The risk with a protected put is that the shares will be "put to you," and you will have to buy them, so you must have enough capital in your account to cover the purchase.

Of course, the key to selling options is to choose a strike price at which you believe the option will expire worthlessly. There is always the risk of being wrong, but if you believe the share price of Facebook, for example, will rise, you could sell a protected $190 put for $4.95, earning $495 per contract. If the stock price rises, the options will expire worthless, allowing you to keep the premium and profit from the transaction.

Naked Puts for Sale

Selling naked puts is a popular strategy among traders with level 4 status. If you can obtain this level from your broker, you should think about this potentially profitable strategy. The key, of course, is to select the appropriate strike price.

When a put is described as "naked," it means it is not backed by anything. However, you are still required by law to fulfill your obligations if the option is exercised, but traders can avoid this problem by purchasing the options back if there is a chance they will be exercised. The time value may work in your favor, making the options cheaper and allowing you to buy them back while still profiting.

Another factor to consider is selecting an option with low implied volatility, which reduces the likelihood that the stock will move significantly during the option's lifetime. However, there is a trade-off here as well, as a few points higher implied volatility can result in a significant increase in the premium received for selling the option.

Take IBM, for example. The stock is currently trading at $139.20, but you could sell a 30-day call option for $139.20.

$135 was exchanged for $2.44, or $244. You could even sell money puts in. A $145 put would sell for $748; if you sold five contracts, you would earn $3,640 in 30 days.

Selling in the money puts could be risky, but beneficial if IBM shares were expected to rise in price. The options will expire worthless if the price rises above the strike price.

While selling LEAPS carries a higher risk due to a long time to expiration, it also provides a higher probability that the option will move in the amount and allows you to sell at high premiums. A $130 put for IBM expiring in 18 months would sell for $13.20, giving you a premium of $6,600 if you sold five contracts. LEAPS can have wide bid-ask spreads, and volume is likely to be below. The bid-ask spread for this option is about 80 cents, which isn't too bad, implying that selling it won't be too difficult. The daily volume is low at 10, but the open interest is high at 1,282. The open interest of 500 or higher is often recommended by experienced traders because it indicates that enough people are buying the contracts.

The risk of naked puts is that you will be forced to purchase the shares. Again, if that appears to be the case, you can purchase the contracts back. Selling out-of-the-money options that expire soon can put you in a better position because the options will most likely expire worthlessly and you will be able to keep the premium without having to buy the options back. If you have to buy the shares, your loss will be equal to the share price minus the market price. Of course, you'd also need the capital to purchase the shares.

So, if you sold a put option on IBM with a strike price of $138 and an expiration date of 6 weeks, you'd get $3.70. If the share price fell to $136, you'd have to use cash to purchase the shares at $138 and risk losing $2 per share if you sold them—or you could simply keep them and wait for the price to riserestore power Furthermore, your loss would be offset by the premium paid, so your break-even point would be the strike price minus the premium paid.

Naked Calls for Sale

Naked calls can also be sold. This means you can sell call options without owning the underlying stock. If the option is exercised, you will have to buy the shares at a higher market price and then sell them at the lower strike price. So the key here is to sell out-of-the-money calls at strike prices that you doubt the stock will reach during the option's lifetime. The same strategies can be used, and if the share price appears to be rising, you can buy back the options to avoid being assigned.Looking at IBM, some modest out-of-the-money call options with 30 days to expiration are available at reasonable prices. A $141 call is $3.55, which is nearly $2 out of the money, so selling one contract would net you $355.

Assume a stock is trading at $195 per share. You could sell a call with a strike price of $200 and a 45-day expiration for $4.46, or $446. If the share price rises to $197 with 10 days to expiration, the calls are now priced at $1.88, or $188. So you could buy them back and still make $258 per contract, avoiding the risk of being assigned if the share price continued to rise. Of course, at $3 out of pocket, you could wait. When the share price rises to $199 with seven days left, the calls will be $218, reducing your profits even further. However, if it fell $1 the next day, the call option would be worth only $1.58.

Remember that when you sell options, you profit from the time premium. In other words, time decay is your friend. Options that are out of the money lose value quickly as the expiration date approaches.

If you can't buy them back, the biggest risk of selling naked call options is having to buy the shares at a high price and then sell them at a loss to meet your obligations. Assume a stock is trading at $95 per share, and you sell a call option with a strike price of $100. Someone might exercise the option if the stock breaks out and rises to, say, $130 per share. Because you sold the call naked, you'd have to buy the shares at $130 and sell them at $130them at the $100 strike price, losing $30 a share, which would be partially offset by the premium, which might be around $1 per share.

So, while selling naked calls can be profitable, it also carries a high level of risk. The key to successfully selling naked calls is to choose the right strike price and a stock that you don't believe will have large enough price movements to cause the option to be in the money.

Brokers may be forced to sell.Most brokerages will automatically exercise options that expire in the money. As a result, you should not let an option expire in the money unless you are prepared to buy or sell the shares as needed.

CHAPTER 24

Success Hints

If you want to start earning money through options trading, there are a few things you should think about before jumping in. Here are a few examples:

Understand When to Leave the Manuscript

While sticking to your plan, even when your emotions tell you to ignore it, is a sign of a successful trader, this does not imply that you must follow it blindly 100 percent of the time. You will, without a doubt, find yourself in a situation where your plan is rendered completely useless by something beyond your control from time to time. You must be aware of your plan's flaws as well as changing market conditions to recognize when following your predetermined course of action will result in failure rather than success. Knowing when the situation is changing versus when your emotions are trying to take control takes practice, but even being aware of the difference is a huge step in the right direction.

Trades that are out of money should be avoided.While there are a few strategies out there that make a point of purchasing options that are currently out of stock, you can rest assured that they are the exception rather than the rule. Remember that the options market is not the same as the traditional stock market, which means that even if you are trading options based on underlying stocks, buying low and selling high is simply not a viable strategy. If a call has dropped out of the money, there is generally less than a 10% chance that it will return to acceptable levels before it expires, which means that purchasing these types of options is little better than gambling, and there are ways to gamble with odds much higher than 10% in your favor.

Never Begin without a Well-Defined Plan for Entry and Exit.More important than establishing entry and exit points, however, is using them even when there appears to be money on the table. One of the most difficult obstacles for new options traders to overcome is the belief that you must squeeze every last penny out of every successful trade. The truth is that as long as you have a profitable trading plan, there will always be more profitable trades in the future, which means that you should be more concerned with protecting the profit that the trade has already netted you. While ignoring this advice may occasionally result in a small profit, the chances are that you will lose far more than you gain as profits peak unexpectedly and begin to fall again before you can effectively pull the trigger.

Read

A minimum of one manuscript per week. It will teach you many things, particularly secrets. It will also give you a better understanding of the risks and rewards.

Trade for Profit, Not for Wealth

If you do this with the expectation of receiving returns of 120 percent, you should reconsider. While a few investments may provide such returns, the vast majority of options will not.

Begin with Enough Funding

One of the first things you should ensure is that you have enough capital to get started with the investment. Capital is the amount of money that you can deposit into your account to help pay for any transactions you chooses, and it can be used if you incur a loss while trading.Always keeps a small amount of money in your trading account. This will come in handy when you're in the middle of a trade and need to make a decision.

It allows your broker to continue working on trades without having to worry about a delay while your funds are transferred.

Avoid the Extremely High Risks

Good options traders don't like a lot of risks, and they don't understand why they should take a big risk for a small chance at a big payout. Rather than pursuing such opportunities, they intend to focus on some trades with high potential but low risk.

Make an effort to diversify.The importance of diversification cannot be overstated. A poorly diversified portfolio is a rookie mistake; however, many professional investors prefer not to diversify due to the way money is managed in the United States.

Try not to freak out.People do not make money by panicking in high-stress situations. There will always be better times to leave or make a move than moves prompted by nervousness or panic. This is the downfall of many people who want to invest but can't seem to master the craft.

Look for the Good in It and Look for Opportunities

The next time you notice a trading situation that has caused a lot of panics; you should immediately take the opposing side. Some of the best trades you can make involve the trade being cleared out as a result of people panicking and using market orders without realizing that the doors for exiting are not as large as they believe or assume.

This is not to say that all of the merchandise that people abandon in a panic is worth investing in overtime. When the market or stocks fall, there is usually a bounce-back that allows you to leave in a better position than if you followed everyone else's lead and left too quickly.

Invest at the Right Times

Because you will learn how to avoid big risks as an options trader, you will learn how to be very careful about your timing when entering and exiting the market. You must be able to read the market correctly to determine the best time to perform both of those tasks. These investors have done their homework and understand how to look at the big picture rather than always calling the broker and hoping they can trust that person.

Learn How to Concentrate.Many people believe that options trading is simple, and then they dive in and become overwhelmed by what they are dealing with. If you are not used to making this type of investment, it may be difficult to deal with at first.If you find that you are unable to easily focus on the task at hand; you may struggle with options trading because you are missing out on opportunities. A trader who can maintain their focus for an extended period is more likely to benefit from this trading style.

Never go along with the crowd.One of the worst things you can do is try to follow the crowd and hope it works out for you. Many beginners find it easy to seek advice from experts, and then they will do exactly what that expert says without doing any research or trusting their judgment. There is nothing wrong with seeking expert advice, but your strategy will not be the same as theirs. You are the only one who knows your limits and your goals, and while you can listen to others' advice, it is important to think for yourself and devise a plan that works for you.Maintain as much simplicity as possible.By definition, options trading is a complex market. You don't need to complicate things any further. Keep your strategies as simple as possible, and make use ofthe most basic technical analysis tools, and manage your money in the most basic way possible The remaining pieces will fall into place on their own.

Avoid overtrading.When dealing with low-cost options, it is very easy to lose track of what you are trading with. Maintain a manageable number of contracts.

Keep an eye on the rankings

Qualification rankings are always available to consult, especially if you are dealing with spreads and especially if you are a novice. A low-ranking option is not a good one, and it will most likely cost you money.

Maintain Consistency

Before you ever make a trade, you should have a good understanding of the strengths and weaknesses of the various stocks in question, as well as the best time to enter a trade and when to exit if things don't go as planned, and also where you will exit if things go as well as you could have hoped. Once you've made a decision, it's critical to stick to it, even if your emotions are urging you to go in a different direction. It is critical to always have faith in your plan because it was created during a time when you were thinking as rationally as possible; giving in to your emotions at this point is akin to gambling with your investments.

Keep the market's mood in mind at all times.Fundamental and technical analysis is useful, but they will only get you so far before the market appears to balk at the logical choice and deviate in an unexpected direction. This typically occurs when the market's will goes against the status quo as a result of an unexpected outpouring of support from traders who are thinking with their guts rather than their brains. The best way to proceed.This is done to keep tabs on what the major players in your market of choice are up to, as this will typically act as a litmus test when it comes to market sentiment.

Maintain a Trading Journal

While it may appear to be a waste of time at first, keeping a journal of all of your trades can be an extremely effective way to analyze what you are doing right and what you are doing wrong when it comes to options trading. While one type of analysis may pique your interest in trading at the moment, keeping a trading journal will allow you to look at your trading results from a more analytical perspective once you've gained some distance and perspective on what you're doing.To get the most out of this process, keep track of each trade you make, as well as the date, the state of the market, and the underlying asset on which you were basing all of your trades, whether the trade was profitable or not, and your emotional and mental state while trading.

These pointers should get you started. With time, you will learn what options to seek and which to avoid. Remember that seasoned traders are those who have been in the business for years, not just a few months.

CHAPTER 25

Predicting Future Directions

The world is full of uncertainty, and the stock market reflects this. Yes, financial instruments are based on so-called fundamentals such as monetary policy, interest rates, and equity fundamentals such as sales and taxes. Market makers are stereotyped as steely-eyed, cold, and calculating automatons. No, they are not. They are human, and they are as emotionally invested in the market as any other investor,'man-on-the-street,' or anyone else. Emotions frequently influence the market as a result of the sometimes irrational reaction to this uncertainty. Recent events such as

Brexit is an example of such an emotional reaction.The Basic Academic Economic Theory assumes that investors act rationally, that is, in the way that best serves their economic interests. Markets do not always act rationally in the real world because humans do not always act rationally.

Certain internal events, such as fund managers establishing positions at the end of the quarter to make their quarterly reports look better, will have an impact on market performance. On Fridays, stock prices and indexes tend to fall as investors prepare for the weekend by taking profits. Predicting market moves can be a lot like reading tea leaves, with a lot of hocus-pocus and mystery. Successful investors, on the other hand, learn or develop a sense of where the market is going and when.

To be successful as an investor, here are five things that must be done. They are fairly obvious, but they must be remembered. The first step is to conduct a Fundamental Analysis. The second step is to conduct technical analysis. They're the meat and potatoes' of trading. The next three, Intuition, Patience, and Attention, are perhaps more important.

Intuition

Many excellent investments can be made using intuition. A family used to take regular vacation trips from Michigan to Florida. They soon noticed a new Cracker Barrel restaurant chain along the interstate highway. When they came to a stop, they had to wait in line, and the food was excellent and reasonably priced. As they made more trips, they noticed that more Cracker Barrel locations were opening, all with the same long wait. They invested in CRBL and watched the stock rise from its entry price of about $5.00 to its current trading range of about $5.00.between $150 and $175 That decision was a great example of trading intuition. CBRL had identified a market niche and filled it with high-quality service and products.

L'eggs has a similar plot. Consumers quickly responded positively to the product's quality and the catchy advertising, which was introduced in 1969. Those L'eggs plastic egg-like containers were a hit with craft workers, propelling Hanes' stock to new highs. Many investors recognized that L'eggs was the right product at the right time, that it was of high quality, and that it had an exciting marketing promotion. This is the essence of successful investing's Intuition component. Look for products that fill a market niche, are of high quality, and are well received by customers.

Patience

Investing in the market, whether through stock purchases and sales or options trading, necessitates patience. Because of uncertainty, an investor may become nervous and make an irrational move. Traders must develop the ability to be patient. No market moves so quickly that a trader cannot make the appropriate trade in response to a change. Keep in mind that options trading is not for the faint of heart. Nervous reactions to unanticipated events can derail a well-planned strategy.

Attention

There is no substitute for keeping an eye on the market and your positions. No, you do not have to watch the big boards every hour of every day. Remember that options trading is not set it and forget its activity. Traders can build very solid portfolios and profit handsomely, but like any other job, the trader must stay current, not just in the market.Not only in market movements, but also in global news and reports. Some resources have enticing features, such as daily free videos on market changes and forecasts from their experts. It is critical to stay current. Some traders will close all positions while on vacation, then resume trading when they return. And, because most people use portable computing devices such as laptops, tablets, smartphones, and so on, they can spend time even while on vacation trading and investing. Whatever route you take, keep in mind that options trading necessitates the investor's undivided attention. Make that decision before you begin.

Traders and analysts can use a variety of tools to forecast what will happen, at least to some extent. On the subject of market forecasting, there are two schools of thought: technical and fundamental methods used by informed investors. The majority of traders use a combination of the two.

Fundamental Examining

Fundamental analysis examines a variety of indicators to determine, at the very least, the direction of the economy, various industry groups, and individual stocks.

It all starts with the overall trend of the economy, both national and global. The adage about a butterfly's flapping wings in Africa causing a hurricane in Florida implies that no national economy exists in a vacuum. There is a great deal of interaction between and among them. When the general economy rises, all individual boats rise, but not necessarily in the same way. Similarly, when the economy suffers, all sectors suffer, but not equally. Some industries will shrink more than others. Sectors such as technology, biotechnology, electronics manufacturing, and cyclical industries such as major appliances and automobiles tend to expand in an expanding economy.

Here are a few more examples of cyclical industries:

Heavy machinery Consumer discretionary goods Tooling and machines Hotels and restaurants Airlines.These stocks typically have a high Beta (), indicating that they react quickly and strongly to changes in the national and global economies.

Non-cyclical industries, such as utilities, consumer staples, energy, and retailers, are relatively safe during downturns. Discount retailers, auto parts retailers, and big-box building suppliers are examples of counter-cyclical businesses that can thrive during economic downturns.

Options prices, crucially for options traders, respond to the volatility and trend of the underlying stocks, so traders must pay close attention to the economic cycle and the sectors of interest to them.Once an investor or options trader has identified the economic trend, such as expanding or contracting, she will focus on a sector of interest such as durable goods, finance, or hospitality, to name a few. She will then examine individual companies within that sector or industry, looking for those that will lead the way. She will do so by assessing the company's business model, business plan, management quality, and financials. Analyst's reports, annual reports, and public commentary can all be used to evaluate business models and business plans. She will assess management quality by examining outcomes, internal business indicators such as return on investment, return on sales, and debt levels to market capitalization. She will read and comprehend the various documents for the firm she is interested in, such as the balance sheet, income or profit and loss statement, cash flow positions, and debt positions. The majority of this information is available online and in public documents, such as annual reports. Annual reports, for example, are written by insiders and may not be completely objective. Various industry analysts and experts may be able to provide more objective perspectives. These are available from brokers and online retailers.

Technical Evaluation

Many investors base their trading decisions on technical factors that combine knowledge of current and historical economic conditions with past performance. This analysis is dominated by looking at charts that show stock performance over time. Using these charts, they can forecast future stock movements and then act on those forecasts by buying and sellingoptions for sale The charts below describe some key market movements that any options trader should be aware of.

The Symmetrical Triangle in Chart 1 depicts a stock trading within a decreasing range. The upper line is a resistance line, and the lower line is a support line. When the price fluctuates between these converging lines, it is frequently an indication of a forthcoming breakout. When there is an upward breakout, the options trader will buy calls to cover a long position in anticipation of the upward swing. If, on the other hand, the pattern suggests that a breakout below the support line is likely, the trader may decide to buy puts in anticipation of a drop in market price.

Triangle Pattern, Chart 1

Triangle patterns can also be oriented upward or downward, indicating whether the stock is likely to rise or fall.

Chart 2: The Triple Crown

The condition depicted in Chart 2 is known as a triple top. The support line is the horizontal dotted line below the chart, and the resistance line is the upper dotted line. The chart depicts the market price making a new low. This is a good time to sell puts. The pattern could have broken upward and crossed the resistance line.It's worth noting that that chart can also be inverted, resulting in a triple bottom. These charts indicate the direction of the stock and help options traders decide whether to trade puts or calls.

Figure 3: The Head and Shoulders

Chart 3 depicts a pattern known as 'head and shoulders.' This pattern differs from a triple top pattern in that the middle peak is usually higher. Head and shoulders patterns can form either upwards or downwards. In any case, it provides an opportunity for options traders. The dotted line represents the most recent support line. This pattern happens to break out downward, but it could very well have broken out upward as well.

Bollinger Bands

Bollinger bands are probability bands that form a ring around a moving average line. These bands are typically set at one or two standard deviations from historical stock prices, which are the closing prices for each day. Movement outside the Bollinger Bands indicates a shift in the underlying stock as a result of market fluctuations. Breaking through the Bollinger Band signals the options trader that it is time to act.

Options traders can benefit from a variety of other technical indicators. The various resources will provide excellent education and insights into basic and advanced analysis techniques. The combination of fundamental and technical analysis is used by the majority of investors and traders, and it is a personal preference. Simply make sure you understand the various indicators and what they can tell you. Use the appropriate tools for each condition. There is no such thing as a "one-size-fits-all" tool; each trader must develop her system of analysis. Intuition, Patience, and Attention are the keys to success.

CHAPTER 26

Trader Emotions

Emotional Investing

It is common for traders to have their emotions and feelings jumbled up when day trading due to the market's highs and lows. This is a far cry from the confident self that a trader usually portrays before the markets open, brimming with anticipation of the

money and profits that they intend to make. Emotions in trading can cloud your judgment and impair your ability to make sound decisions. Day trading should not be done without emotion, but rather as a trader. You should be able to work your way around them and make them work for you. Whether your profits are increasing or decreasing, you should maintain a clear, levelheaded, and stable mind at all times. This is not to say that you should disconnect from your emotions as a trader. Emotions cannot be avoided, but when confronted with real-world market scenarios, you must learn how to work through and around them. A trader's personality type has a significant impact on the type of trader they are. When it comes to opening trades, cautious traders are mostly controlled by fear, whereas risky traders are driven by greed. Fear and greed are such powerful motivators that they can go a long way the way in the arrangement of losses and profits

Greed

A trader may be motivated to earn more money after checking their account balances and discovering that it is at a low level. While this may be a motivator to work hard, some traders take it too far, expecting to earn a large sum of money right away. They make mistakes in trading that have the opposite effect of what they intended. Overtrading and taking unnecessary risks are examples of such mistakes.

Unnecessary Risk-Taking

Greed for more money will try to persuade the trader to take unnecessary risks to reach a certain financial threshold in the trading account. These will almost certainly result in losses. Risky traders may take risks such as high leverage, which they hope will work in their favor but may result in massive losses.

Performing an Overtrade

A trader may trade for extended periods due to the desire to make more and more money. Often, these efforts are futile, because overtrading through market highs and lows puts a trader in a position where their accounts can be wiped out as a result of greed. Taking into account the time of trading and jumping into opening trades without doing analysis will almost certainly result in a loss.

Inadequate Profit and Loss Understanding

Wanting to make a lot of money in a short period will cause a trader to not close a losing trade, keeping the losses, and on the other hand, overriding on a profitable trade until the market reverses, canceling out all the gains made. It is best to maximize and specialize in a winning trade and close a losing trade as soon as possible to avoid major losses.

Fear

Fear can act in both directions, acting as a limit to overtrading as well as a limit to profit-making. A trader may close a trade to avoid a loss, which is motivated by fear. A trader may also close a trade too soon, even if it is on a winning streak, in fear that the market will reverse and result in losses. Fear is the motivator in both scenarios, working to avoid failure while also achieving success.

The Fear of Failure

The fear of failing in trading may prevent a trader from opening trades and simply watching the market change and move in cycles while doing nothing. The fear of losing money in trading is a deterrent to success. It prevents a trader from carrying out what could have been a profitable transaction.

The Fear of Success

This type of fear in trading psychology will cause a trader to give up profits to the market when there is an opportunity to do so. In market scenarios, it has a self-destructive effect. Such traders in this category are afraid of making too much profit and allow losses to run, despite being aware of their activities and the losses they will incur.

Trading Dishonesty

There are several market biases that a trader may develop as a result of an emotional play, which traders are advised to avoid. These biases in trading psychology may influence a trader to make unwise and uncalculated trading decisions that may prove to be loss-making. Even when your trading biases are in focus, you must be aware of your emotions as a trader and devise ways to keep them in check while maintaining a cool head in your trading window. Together with the underlying cause of all of them: fear. Overconfidence, confirmation, anchoring, and loss are examples of biases.

Overconfidence Bias

It is common for traders, especially new traders, to experience euphoria in the state of winning after making a large profit on a trade. You want to keep opening trades, believing that your analysis can't go wrong, all the way down to the profits and gains you've made. This should not be happening. You can't be so excited and confident in your analysis skills that you believe you can't lose. Because the market is volatile, the cards can change at any time, and when they do, the over-excited and overconfident trader becomes a disappointing one. Before opening any trade, conduct a thorough market analysis, regardless of whether the previous trades were a loss or a win.

Bias in Trade Confirmation

In trading psychology, one of the factors that wastes a lot of time and money for traders is the bias in confirmation of a trade you have already made, justifying it. Professional traders are more likely to exhibit this type of bias. They return to evaluating and analyzing trades after making them.They simply made, attempting to demonstrate that it was the correct one, whether they sailed according to the market. They squander a lot of time digging for information that they already know. They could also be demonstrating that the mistake they made in opening a bad trade and making a bad move was correct. Nonetheless, confirmation bias kicks in when a trade they made turns out to be correct, and this strengthens their resolve in their research skills, leading them to waste even more time proving to themselves already known facts. They may also lose money in the process, so it is best to avoid this type of bias in trading.

Anchoring on Obsolete Strategies Leads to Bias

This type of bias in trading psychology applies to traders who rely on outdated information and strategies that do more harm than good to their trading success. Anchoring on correct but irrelevant information when trading may expose the trader to losses, which is a setback for traders who are always too lazy to look for new market information. One of the most important aspects of having a successful trading career is keeping up with current events and factors that may have an impact on the market. Lazy traders will grow tired of keeping up with current economic and even political events that have an impact on the foreign exchange market. As an example, some traders may lose a trade, but they hope that the markets will reverse their assumptions based on outdated information and strategies. Conduct extensive research, keeping in mind that it should not take too much time, to ensure that you make trades based on accurate information.

Bias in Loss Avoidance

Trading to avoid losses usually boils down to the fear factor. Some traders' trading patterns and trading windows are dictated by their fear of losing money. Gains and profits are not motivators for them when fear prevents them from opening trades that could have been profitable. They also close their trades too soon, even when they are profitable, to avoid their imaginable losses. After conducting a thorough market analysis, go for profits rather than being discouraged by the bias of avoiding losses, which only serves to hold many traders back. Come up with somethingwith a plan for your day trading to deal with doubts about the trades, you'll be making

Traders' Habits Are Influenced by Psychology

A trader's trading habits, mistakes, and winning strategies are all influenced by psychological factors. The following sections explain the negative habits that many traders have, as well as the influence of psychology on their habits.

Trading without a Plan

A trader will face difficulties if he or she does not have a trading strategy and plan to refer to. A trader should develop a proper strategy to use as a reference point when dealing with a problem in the market. It should be a well-thought-out plan that outlines what to do in specific situations and which trading patterns to employ in various case scenarios. Trading without a strategy is the same as trading to lose money.

Inadequate Financial Management Plans

Money management plans are one of the most important aspects of trading, and without solid strategies in this area, it is difficult to progress in making profits on trades opened. As a trader, you must follow certain principles that will guide you in how to spend your money in the account to open trades and ensure profits. Without money management plans, a trader would be trading blindly with no end goal in mind, putting money at risk in losing trades.

Desire to Be Always Correct

Some traders always trade against the market, expressing their desire for the market to behave in a certain way. They do not follow the market signal, but rather their philosophy, not doing proper analysis and always wanting to be right. Such psychological habits result in losses. When the trading window closes, the market always takes precedence over the traders. As a result, a trader's desire to always be right against the market is overruled.

CHAPTER 27

Management of Money

What Exactly Is Money Management?

Money management refers to how you manage your finances, including your savings, spending, and investments. It is ensuring that you will be able to survive a financial crisis. It entails creating a budget for your

long-term goals, as well as making investments that will help you achieve your goals. You will be able to make wise purchases if you manage your money well.

Otherwise, no matter how much money you make, you will always complain about having less. It is also referred to as investment management.

Money management is more concerned with risk. You can reduce your risk by improving your money management skills. To avoid risks, you must understand all aspects of money management. Plan with a negative bias, always considers "what-if" scenarios, act, and plan. When creating a budget for money management, make sure you spend less than you save. Excellent money management will assist you in monitoring your spending and preventing you from exceeding your budget. You will secure your savings by doing so.

If you make the right choices, you will be able to invest. Avoiding additional risks will assist you in meeting your financial objectives. The strategies you employ in your investments are critical to your success. When deciding to invest, the first thing to consider is the risk involved, and how to avoid it. Here are some of the fundamentals, benefits, and drawbacks of money management.

Money Management Fundamentals

Money management is a broad term that encompasses solutions and services throughout the investment industry. In today's market, you can find a variety of resources as well as phone applications to help you manage all of your finances. A financial advisor can also help investors manage their money professionally. Financial advisors collaborate with private banking and even brokerage firms to provide money management plans that include services such as retirement and estate planning.

The Benefits of Financial Management

Improved Money Management

When you have a good budget, you can track how you spend your money and keep track of every expense. This is a significant benefit to you because it allows you to spend less and save more money. Monitor your expenses for a few months, then change your budgeting by eliminating less necessary expenses and allocating that money to a savings plan, a retirement plan, or a vacation fund. Excellent money management will assist you in staying on track; you will be able to pay your bills on time, stay within your budget, and avoid bank account overdrafts. Poor financial management can put you in debt in the blink of an eye. When you go over your limit, you can avoid those pesky fees. You will avoid overspending if you have a good budget.

A Sound Retirement Strategy

Better financial management and savings plans will benefit you in the long run. You will be able to plan for your retirement and secure your future. Better money management skills will provide you with a better retirement plan. No matter how much you save, even if you only save and invest a small amount of money, it will provide you with a larger sum for your retirement later in life.

Mindfulness

You will have peace of mind if you manage your money properly. Having bills on the counter and no idea how to pay them, or not having enough money to buy something you needed. All of these issues can be difficult to deal with daily. Managing your money wisely and experiencing everything

You will have peace of mind as a result of good money management, and you will be able to provide for yourself and your family.

The Drawbacks of Money Management

Rapid Transitions

Because of the rapid changes in the financial world, it is necessary to change your management plans regularly. It can be difficult to adjust your plans to account for rapidly changing circumstances. Your plan will be limited unless it can assist in the adoption of new techniques.

Time-Consuming

Managing your money can be a time-consuming task at times. It necessitates that you make the most accurate estimates possible. However, you can use software and mobile applications to help you plan, which may save you time compared to if you didn't use the technologies. And if you don't know much about money management, it will take you longer to get there.

Inaccuracy

In terms of estimating your expenses, you make a lot of assumptions when planning. Any change, such as an economic downturn or a change in the currency rate or interest rates, can cause your planning estimates to change.

What Is the Importance of Money Management?

When money is well-managed, it becomes a wealth. It is a tool that is used to acquire wealth. For wealthy people, having and spending money does not bring them joy; what brings them joy is having a steady income and being able to continue achieving their goals—and being able to leave a legacy to their loved ones. Money management is concerned with your habits, and your decisions can have an impact on the outcome of your long-term strategies. There are many powerful elements in the pursuit of wealth, such as debts, risks, and taxes, that can undo all of your hard work to achieve your goals. This is a life skill that everyone should acquire. You don't have to be a financial expert to begin managing your money. There is plenty of it.

There is a wealth of information available to assist you in better understanding your finances. The following are some of the reasons why money management is important:

Defining clear objectives. To build your wealth, take a clear approach to your money management decisions. Making the best decision will get you closer to your objectives. Set some clear and realistic goals for yourself, as well as a time frame for achieving them. Setting clear goals will allow you to track where you are and see your progress toward your goals. Some people give up too soon because they can't see their progress. If you divide your goals into short-term milestones, you will be able to see your progress and stay motivated. Finally, set clear and quantifiable goals to assist you in making sound decisions. Abandon any options that will not bring you closer to your goal.

Managing your cash flow. Spending less than you earn will assist you in accumulating wealth. You cannot be financially successful unless you track and monitor your expenses. Making a spending plan and sticking to it religiously may appear trivial, but it is critical to the success of the world's wealthiest people. If you own a business, your goal will be to increase your monthly profits, which you will use to invest in further growth. When you have a solid money management plan and make the right decisions, you will learn how to prioritize your spending and get closer to your goals.

Creating a budget Making a household income budget is an important part of personal financial management. Budgeting will assist you in better understanding your cash flow, providing you with a clear picture of your current financial situation.

Debt administration. There is proper financial education available to assist you in understanding consumer debt and how it works. There are also financial advisers and credit counselors who can advise you on how to review your debts, loan terms, and how to pay off the debt quickly and without stress.

Take care of your risks. As you continue to amass wealth, your risk exposure grows. Wealth, contrary to popular belief, does not make life easier. The unspoken truth is that it

can make life more difficult Buying a bigger house, expensive cars, and living a lavish lifestyle. These involve financial risk and the possibility of loss if everything goes well.

Include a risk management assessment in your financial plan, as well as protection strategies, to help you prepare for the unexpected. Among the unintended consequences are:

Income loss as a result of illness or an accident The death of the family's breadwinner Assets is vulnerable to liability claims.

Money management will give you a 360-degree view of your financial situation, and financial discipline will help you overcome these obstacles. You will have better control over your financial goals if you follow a solid money management principle.

Being fiscally responsible. Taxation is a responsibility; however, there is no obligation to pay more than is required. Most people are unaware of how much tax they are paying, the consequences of the unnecessary taxes, and how this affects their ability to accumulate wealth. Money management is concerned with what you receive after paying your taxes rather than what you make. Your investment's tax characteristics, as well as the tax characteristics of your overall portfolio, must be considered. The first thing to consider is account location, which is the allocation of funds on various types of accounts based on their respective tax treatment. Second, asset location, in which you allocate different types of investments among various types of accounts based on tax treatment—for example, allocating your least tax-efficient assets to a tax-deferred account such as 401(k) (k). Taxable accounts can invest in tax-advantaged investments such as low turnover funds. This will give you more options for income distribution in a more tax-efficient retirement, allowing you to accumulate more wealth faster.

CHAPTER 28

Errors and Mistakes in Trading

When you trade options, you typically profit when the underlying stock moves sideways, up, or down. Options strategies are an excellent way to generate and protect profits while avoiding losses.You can control significant portions of stock with a small cash outlay, but all of this sounds too good to be true because there is a catch.Trading options can cause you to lose more money than you put in in a short period. This is why it is critical to proceed with caution and care. Even experienced traders can make simple mistakes that have serious consequences.

People can make a lot of money by trading options. It is critical to trade options correctly and avoid making mistakes that could result in a large loss. It is advisable to keep a list of common blunders that occur when attempting to become an advanced trader. Many of these errors are similar to those made by inexperienced traders. As a result, many traders tend to lose their entire account right away. However, the majority of these errors are simple enough to avoid. Let's take a look at the various errors and mistakes to avoid when trading options. You should keep these things in mind at all times because they will help you earn a lot of money while avoiding losses.Short time frames should be avoided.

Many options brokers have begun to offer a wide range of time frames in recent years. Nowadays, many brokers offer users extremely short contact periods; in fact, many brokers offer a minute-long contact period. These times of the year tend to attract new users who have no prior trading experience. They can, however, attract experienced traders looking to make a quick buck. If statistics are used to make a decision,

When examined closely, it is clear that this novel approach is a fad that can lead to major problems. Markets are impossible to forecast, and no one can predict what will happen in the next minute or so. As a result, these options contacts should be avoided at all costs. Do not pursue them because they will undoubtedly result in a loss.

Even in larger time frames such as months and weeks, the market is difficult to predict, but in the case of longer time frames, traders can generally assess the dominant trends. They can also take a position that recognizes and reflects the state of the options market.

Utilize Moderate Leverage Levels

Using excessive leverage is another simple mistake that can be avoided. This can happen in a variety of ways. For example, some traders who are losing money begin to look for new strategies to compensate for their losses. Doubling-up occurs when traders add new positions at higher or lower levels (depending on the direction of the original trade). This phrase is frequently thought to be a more polite and diplomatic version of 'adding to a loser,' which describes the same phenomenon.

Many other errors can be seen when traders use very little margin in their positioning. This opens up the possibility of significant profits, but it also exposes a trading account to extreme losses if the market fails to move in the desired direction. These are just a few of the many reasons why it is always better to avoid chasing after quick profits and instead work hard. It is advised to take a conservative but functional approach that limits leverage levels on an average scale.

Make Use of an Economic Calendar

Many trading failures can occur when a trader uses an economic calendar before creating and establishing new market positions. It is critical to understand that for any tradable asset, there are always relevant events that can result in shocking and unexpected volatility in future prices. These events vary depending on the type of asset being traded at the time. People who trade stock options or deal with stock benchmarks, for example, must have a proper educationunderstanding of when major earnings reports are released In most cases, this leads to increased volatility inequities. It is difficult to predict where this volatility will go in the future. As a result, it is generally a wise strategy to wait for major news events to pass before deciding to establish market positions. Most of these events are usually planned ahead of time, so keeping an economic calendar handy is a good idea. If used wisely, it will prove to be a valuable asset to all traders.

Concentrate on Liquid Assets

For some, this is contentious advice, but it is recommended to focus on liquid assets. Many options traders look for opportunities in assets that aren't as widely traded as others. These types of trades have the potential to generate a sizable profit. However, if you want to maintain a conservative outlook and reduce the likelihood of risks, you should consider liquid assets. Liquid assets will allow you to avoid risks while still profiting. The most common and frequently traded assets are liquid assets. Stock benchmarks, blue-chip stocks, silver, gold, oil, and forex majors such as EUR/USD, USD/GBP, USD/JPY, and AUD/USD are examples of these.

Always have an exit strategy in place.You must learn how to control and manipulate your emotions when you enter the world of finance and trading. This does not imply that you should abandon all emotions and become a fearless being. Instead, you should make a plan and try to stick to it as much as possible. You must have an exit strategy.

Before you begin trading, you must have a backup plan or an exit strategy. If you plan to invest a large sum of money in trading and do not have an exit strategy in place, you may suffer massive losses. People who use American-style options trading must have an exit strategy. It is required because, in this style, traders are allowed to close the position before the contract expires automatically. Because the market is volatile and constantly changing, no trade can guarantee you a 100 percent chance of success. This means that traders must be prepared for a variety of scenarios, particularly when markets do not follow the expected or planned trajectory

You may have never used an exit strategy before and still done well in the past, but there is nothing worse than losing a large sum of money because you are unable to exit the market. The most successful options traders have a plan in place for every possible scenario. To begin, you must examine and develop an exit strategy before the market begins to work against you.

You must define a downside exit point, an upside exit point, and all timeframes for all other exits when things are going well.It is recommended to create an upside exit strategy as well as a worst-case scenario downside exit strategy. If you achieve your upside targets, you should close your positions as soon as possible. Don't be too greedy. Clear your positions as soon as you reach your downside loss step. Do not allow yourself to incur additional losses by gambling your options by waiting for the price to rise again.Because circumstances change so frequently, many people tend to avoid this advice. However, do not do it. Make a plan and try to stick to it as much as you can. Many traders make a plan, then abandon it in favor of following their emotions. It might work a couple of times, but it could lead to massive losses in the long run.

Call Options (OTM)

Buying OTM or out of the money calls outright is a difficult way to make money in options trading, even though it may sound appealing to beginners and some experts because it is extremely cost-effective and appears efficient. Buying them cheaply allows you to spend your money on a variety of other things. Many people believe that this is a safe option because it corresponds with the pattern that people who engage in equity trading are accustomed to. This pattern, i.e., buying low and selling high, can be found almost anywhere. However, if you only use this strategy, you will severely limit yourself and may begin losing money regularly.Try selling the OTM call option on a stock you already own. This should be your first plan of action. It is known as a covered call in the trading worldstrategy.

The best part about the covered call strategy is that the risk factor does not arise from selling the option when it is covered by a stock position. It also has a lot of potentials to help you earn money on stocks when you want to sell the stock when its price rises. This strategy is great because it allows you to 'feel' how the prices of OTM option contracts fluctuate all the time, especially when the expiration date is approaching quickly. Stock prices fluctuate as a result of such events.

However, there is a significant risk in owning the stock. Selling the call option does not create capital risks in and of itself, but it does limit your upside. This means that it will create a risk of missed opportunities. Another risk arises if you intend to sell the stock upon assignment if the market rises. Your decision is then put into action.

Misinterpretation of Leverage

You'd be surprised to learn that many advanced traders overlook the leverage factor option. Many people abuse this contract option because they do not realize how much risk they are taking as a result of it. They frequently purchase short-term calls.

It is suggested that you become a master of leverage. It should be your top priority, especially if you are a beginner looking to enter the advanced strategy. Instead of considering a large number of shares if you typically trade 100 share lots, consider only one share. Similarly, if you typically trade 400 share lots, limit yourself to 4 contracts. This is a good starting point. If you don't succeed in these sizes, you'll almost certainly fail in the larger ones.

Unwillingness to Try New Approaches

Accepting change can help you become a more successful person in general. Many options traders believe that buying out-of-the-money options or never selling in-the-money options is a bad idea that should be avoided at all costs. These may appear to be childish strategies until you are caught in a trade that is being moved against you.Every experienced options trader has been through this before. This scenario can be challenging, which is why many people attempt to break itrules and work in opposition to them

CHAPTER 29

How to Make a Million Using Options Trading

Trading Strategies That Are Extremely Profitable in Any Market Condition

Most investors and traders in the securities markets hope to make a profit by buying low and selling high. Options traders, on the other hand, are the most important layers in any market. This is due to their ability.Earn a lot of money regardless of the market conditions.

Options traders can profit in any market condition, even if there are no trades up or down. The reason for this is that options contracts are flexible in various ways. This adaptability is what makes them such effective market tools for long-term profitability. Here are some profitable strategies you can use.

Alternatives for writing.Writing options are one of the best ways to win at options. You can create some pretty sophisticated strategies that can earn you a lot of money.

As a writer, you have the opportunity to earn a premium. This is money that you earn even if the investor never uses it. It is entirely possible to write profitable commodity-based options regularly. Profitable options that speculators believe will perform well in the options markets can be developed.

The Straddle Plan

This is yet another strategy for making money with options trading. The majority of options involve the purchase of security that becomes profitable when the underlying commodity moves in a specific direction. It could be up or down, but the movement is all that is required. A straddle is an excellent option investment vehicle because it does not require a specific outcome, as in other situations.

A straddle allows you to buy both calls and put options with the same expiry dates and strike times. The straddle strategy can succeed if and only if the underlying security of the option moves in either direction, as long as the movement is large enough to cover the cost of premiums in both directions. Speculators can write straddle options if they believe the market will reward them.

The Collar Approach

There is also a strategy known as the collar strategy. It is regarded as a difficult option strategy to comprehend. A seasoned speculator, on the other hand, can write one for you if he owns the underlying asset. He can take the risk because he owns the asset.

In this case, an out-of-the-money put option is the best option. This is advantageous because, because it is a put option, the losses will be minimal if the commodity price falls. However, if the commodity rises in price, the trader will profit handsomely.

The Strangle Plan

The strangle strategy is similar to the straddle strategy in some ways. This is because they both include the purchase of a call and put option, as well as the same expiration date. The only difference is that their strike prices are different. For speculators, the information available can be used to enter a low-cost position.

When a trader or speculator chooses this strategy, they choose a low-cost entry because either or both options contracts can be purchased out-of-the-money. As a result, it may not be worthwhile to exercise the right provided by the shares. A speculator or even a trader can write the straddle or strangle.So, which option strategy is the most profitable?

We've now looked at a variety of options trading strategies, all of which are profitable and simple to implement. Options trading techniques come in over 40 different varieties. This makes determining the most profitable options trading strategy a difficult task.

Traders frequently seek out trades that will not result in a loss of capital. Furthermore, there are many differing viewpoints on the best and most profitable strategies. Fortunately, the majority of options trading strategies provide very attractive returns, with large margins being quite common. However, it can be a risky venture, so proceed with caution even if your goal is to become a wealthy millionaire.Options trading is extremely profitable.Some people are concerned about the profitability of options trading as well as the risks it entails. Fortunately, it has proven to be quite profitable over the years.Trade-in options give you leverage and the inherent right to control a large number of shares. This type of leverage provides far greater returns than simply selling stocks can.

If you can take advantage of the leverage provided by stock options, you have a good chance of making a lot of money. Profits are made from minuscule movements in the underlying stocks. You will be able to make money regardless of market conditions if you identify the right strategies.This entails profiting even when the market is not moving. However, with some strategies, you could lose money if you make a bad decision. As a result, adequate precautions must be taken to mitigate any such losses, which can be significant.

Options Trading Strategy That Is Most Profitable

It is best to start with the most fundamental options trading strategies. This is how the majority of options traders begin. You can make huge returns on your investments by using these simple options trading strategiestrading abilities It is very possible to achieve a 100 percent return on investment in a matter of days, and sometimes even in a matter of hours.There are also numerous websites and advisory services that offer traders advice and trading assistance. Some transactions may fail. However, the majority of your trades are likely to be successful. As a result, a good approach to this challenge would be to place multiple trades on each occasion. Make sure your strategy will make you money even if one or two trades lose money.

Selling Puts and Credit Spreads Are Consistently Profitable Strategies

According to some credible studies, the two most profitable options trading strategies are selling credit spreads and selling put options. The study discovered that the profits from such trades are consistent and consistent over a long period.The study, however, discovered something else. According to the study, buying call-and-put options is more profitable in the long run, despite being less consistent. You can expect to earn 7 percent to 12 percent per month on the total portfolio, which equates to 84 percent to more than 144 percent per year. Given that the techniques used are very simple, easy to apply, and only require the most basic of technical analysis, your chances of making money without stress are extremely high. If you develop the right trading strategy, you can expect to win more than 80% of your trades.

Overall, the most effective options trading strategy

According to findings, it is widely accepted that selling puts yields the highest profits. If you put a large portion of your trading capital into selling put options, you stand to make a lot of money consistently and with little risk of loss.The only disadvantage of the selling option is that it has some limitations. This is because selling put options works best in a market that is trending upwards or on the rise. For long-term contracts, you can supplement selling puts with selling ITM puts. These are six-month or longer contractslonger. They will make you a lot of money simply because of the time decay effect.Furthermore, as an options trader, you will be able to profit from the market in both directions if you sell credit spreads. This means that you will profit from both upward and downward market trends. This is fantastic because it allows even inexperienced traders to profit. As a result, always remember not to look for the size of the profits. When looking for the most profitable and successful options strategy, consider the following factors:

Capability to devise a dependable and secure plan Have a plan in place to generate consistent income. The risks are minimal.Technical requirements can be met.One of the most profitable ways to make money trading options is to sell naked puts. The margin return is nearly as lucrative as selling credit spreads. It does not, however, carry the same level of risk. In short, when you sell a put option, you open up the possibility of purchasing a stock at a price of your choosing.

Taking a Closer Look at Naked Puts

It's the end of June, and XYZ stock is currently trading at $50. However, the market is volatile, and you would prefer to purchase this stock for $45. At this point, you need to sell a $45 put option for $2. This option's expiration date can be set to the third week of July. You will receive $200 into your trading account as soon as you post the option. If the XYZ stock price falls below $45, you will be forced to buy 100 units. This will set you back $4,500.

However, because you already have $200 in your account, the cost of purchasing the shares is reduced by $200. You will receive $1,200 if you sell a put option every month for the next six months. This will significantly reduce the cost of purchasing XYZ stock.

However, if the stock begins to rise, you will not need to buy it and will instead continue to sell the put option. While there is a slight risk due to liquidity issues, this strategy is quite successful and can lead to enormous profits in a short period.

Return on Investment (ROI) is an abbreviation for Return on Investment

The Expression ROI is an abbreviation for Return on Investment. ROI is a performance indicator that is used by both investors and traders to assess the effectiveness and efficiency of an investment. This includes any trading capital you may have. ROI is a deliberate attempt to directly measure the total return derived from a specific investment.

For example, if you invest a total of X on a specific trade and then receive a return of Y, ROI will attempt to indicate the performance of your investment amount and what you received for your efforts. To calculate the rate of return on investment, first determine the total return, which is then divided by the investment amount.

The profitability of your investment portfolio is one of the most important aspects to consider. You must monitor your investments regularly, which is best accomplished through the use of the ROI, or return on investment. It is advisable to calculate the return on investment for each dollar invested. This figure can be calculated using a formula.

Return on Investment = (Profits – Costs) / Costs

Even so, investors should be aware that the ROI is affected by a variety of other factors, such as the type of investment security chosen, and so on. Also, keep in mind that a high ROI indicates a higher risk, whereas a low figure indicates a lower risk. As a result, proper risk management must be implemented.